PRAISE FOR
Outside the Lines

"The intersection of heartbreak and humor: that's the sweet spot that Helen Fremont nails with such devastating effect in her new memoir *Outside the Lines*."

—Richard Russo, author of *Empire Falls* and the *North Bath Trilogy* series

"Over four heartrending, transformative years, Helen Fremont lives through all the big questions—love, family, art, caretaking, death, self-knowledge—as an impossible situation just keeps getting more impossible. Where there are no answers and no solutions, Fremont offers tenderness, self-deprecating humor, wisdom, and most powerfully, a deep and abiding love that honors not just Maddie, but the power of seeing and being seen by our own beloveds."

—Caitlin Horrocks, author of *Life Among the Terranauts* and *The Vexations*

"Helen Fremont has written a rich, moving story of coming out: as a lesbian in the conservative 1980s; as a daughter starting to resist parental demands; and as a woman learning the complexities of intimacy and mortality."

—Margo Jefferson, author of *Negroland* and *Constructing a Nervous System*

"Long before words like 'adulting' or 'throuple' entered contemporary parlance, Helen Fremont was a young lawyer negotiating romance (in an era still largely unenlightened about same-sex love) and forming an identity (despite a shaky understanding of her past). Enter a love affair with a married friend and a devastating health diagnosis to create an atypical story of responsibility, ambition, and love. I started this book when I had other things to do, but then couldn't put it down, so read in a single sitting, completely absorbed by the heartbreaking story, the whip-smart writing, and the funny, fearless author."

—Debra Spark, Author of *Discipline* and *Breaking Bread*

"By turns deeply funny and deeply sad, Helen Fremont has written a moving and engrossing love story."

—Helen Epstein, author of *The Long Half-Lives of Love and Trauma*

"In *Outside the Lines* best-selling memoirist Helen Fremont delivers a profound history lesson as she deftly weaves the many ways the past confines our ability to love in the present. What were the risks and rewards of queer life outside of the constraints of youth, heterosexual marriage, and illness. I felt I had entered a new genre of memoir, one filled with sizzling passion and need as queer bodies discover real desire for the first time. Fremont makes us look back at our own histories and gives us all the permission to forgive ourselves for not knowing how to love but doing it anyway."

—P. Carl, author of *Becoming a Man: The Story of a Transition*

PRAISE FOR HELEN FREMONT'S
After Long Silence

"A triumphant work of art ... [a] harrowing account... an incredible tale of survival, a beautiful love story, and a suspenseful account of how the author's investigation of her roots shattered fiercely guarded family secrets."

—*Publishers Weekly* (starred review)

"A deeply moving family memoir ... an immensely gifted writer who has vividly reconstructed a sensitive and memorable family saga of terror, hiding, and passing, as well of personal imperatives over two generations around both casting off and confronting the past."

—*Kirkus Reviews* (starred review)

"Poignant ... affecting ... part detective story, part literary memoir, part imagined past."

—*The New York Times Book Review*

"Riveting ... painfully authentic... a poignant memoir, a labor of love for the parents she never really knew"

—*The Boston Globe*

PRAISE FOR HELEN FREMONT'S
The Escape Artist

Outside the Lines

A Memoir

HELEN FREMONT

Sibylline
DIGITAL FIRST

Author's Note

This is a work of nonfiction. I have changed the names and some details of a number of individuals in order to protect their privacy. Like all personal narratives, mine is inherently subjective. I have relied on my notes, journal entries, and memory—however susceptible to errors of fact and interpretation—to tell my story as truthfully as I can.

For Donna, always

CHAPTER 1

In those days I used to wake before dawn, bike across town to the Boys and Girls Club and swim a mile in the dimly lit pool, chanting the number of each lap to empty my mind. Then I'd head downtown to work as a staff attorney at the public defender's office. I'd return home at night to my water-stained, rent-controlled apartment that I shared with a large family of cockroaches. At twenty-nine, I still had the mind of a teenager, the direct result of being my parents' daughter. In our family, growing up—assuming independence—was taboo. Despite outward appearances of holding down a job, paying the rent, foraging for food, and getting myself to therapy on time, I was fundamentally a kid attached to my parents at the expense of knowing who I was.

Of course, my parents had no idea who I was either. Their lives had been shattered by the war, their dreams amputated. I was their new limb. It had never been any of my business what I thought or wanted. I did my best to fit into the image my parents projected of me, contorting myself to catch the beam of light in their eyes. It took me decades to separate my own feelings and desires from theirs.

1987 turned out to be a big year for me, development-wise. In January I finally tested my long-held theory that I was probably queer by sleeping with, and (to my surprise) falling in love with a woman named Carla. An older married woman, as it turned out, with a husband and two kids, but this didn't seemed like such a bad idea, since I was not looking for commitment. I was already in a committed relationship with my parents and sister. I figured a married woman would place fewer demands on me.

My affairs with men had always left me wishing for less. It hadn't occurred to me that changing the gender of the person I slept with would revolutionize the intensity of my feelings and needs. Such is the awesome power of denial.

I also decided that year to return to my first love—writing. It had claimed me since the age of six, when I'd first picked up a pencil and put words on paper. *Any words I wanted!* This love affair had continued until college, when, with the help of my parents, I renounced recreational writing as frivolous and self-indulgent, in favor of the more depressing goal of getting a career.

Now, finally, self-indulgence sounded good to me. I told my mother I'd signed up for a fiction workshop that summer. "Whatever for?" she said. "You'll never win the Pulitzer!"

No one could accuse my mother of being unrealistic.

"I just want to do it for fun," I said. In our family, of course, this was ignoble. It was ok to have fun as a *by-product* of a selfless and honorable endeavor, but it was considered low-brow and hedonistic to apply oneself (and one's money) to doing something *just for the fun of it.* I was disappointed but not surprised by my mother's reaction, and accepted the shame of embarking on a journey of which she disapproved.

I knew better than to mention that I was seeing a woman; I was not yet ready to give up my mother for good.

★ ★ ★

Our fiction workshop of ten women met on Tuesday and Thursday evenings that summer at Harvard. We sat around a large table in the Woodberry Poetry Room of the library. Stratis, our teacher, had a melodious Greek accent, jet-black hair, a dashing mustache, and a twinkle in his eye. We spent an hour on each student's story (two per evening) discussing, parsing, and puréeing the work while the author, herself, remained silent. Then Stratis would sweep us up on the flying carpet of his mind, weaving art, literature, history, psychology, craft, and structure together with his comments on the student's work. Finally the author was allowed to make a brief comment or two, before we turned to the next story.

Writing workshops, in general, are a crap shoot, but that summer's class was magic. We just clicked, a connection that led to years of meeting in one another's apartments, workshopping our stories, growing stronger as writers and closer as friends. But back then we knew nothing of that future, only the court and spark of those two evenings a week.

My classmate Maddie Brinley was runway-model tall and lithe; head poised on the pedestal of her neck like a Modigliani figure. Delicate features, surprisingly full lips, and greenish brown eyes that seemed mysterious, slightly off-center.

It was her hands that got to me, those long slender fingers set off by a man's leather-banded watch on one wrist and a wide-cuff silver bracelet on the other. Shirt collar thrown open, sleeves rolled carelessly below the elbow. Sometimes she wore her dark shoulder-length hair tied back or wrapped in a colorful turban. Even in jeans or cargo pants, she looked elegant and classy, with crazy good posture. Across the table from her, I was a sloucher; a lap swimmer and gym rat, built low to the ground like a creeping weed. Maddie was a cypress. I figured she was about my age, maybe a little older, but in fact she was fully ten years older, with two kids already in grade school.

In class she seemed reserved at first, a bit reticent. When she spoke, her words arranged themselves into clear, intelligent paragraphs. I, on the other hand, was always chasing my thoughts all over the hills, talking a blue streak and hoping someone would stop me before anyone got hurt.

She also struck me as benignly straight. I imagine she saw me as simply dowdy—I came to class directly from work, wearing atrociously cheap suits from Filene's Basement, pantyhose and black Puma sneakers. (In my office I always changed into flat-heeled pumps, and I'd once come upon my boss and the General Counsel pretending to throw my black Pumas out the sixth-floor window.) I wore fuss-free short dark hair, no make-up, no jewelry, no purse; I hauled my stuff around in a mountaineering daypack. Any queer person could have spotted me as a dyke at fifty paces, but in the 1980's, straight people didn't seem to have access to even the most rudimentary gaydar.

I, on the other hand, was all aquiver with gaydar, having recently burst from my chrysalis into a rainbow of lesbian adolescence. I now saw the entire world shimmer through lavender-tinted glasses. A quick sweep of the Woodberry Poetry Room on the first evening told me I was the only queer in class, something I had come to expect in most rooms I entered, although I was sensitized to pick up even the slightest trace of DP. The Dyke Potential here was low, but I did spot a few candidates for the IBTC (Itty-Bitty Titty Committee), whose members often showed a correlation with DP, but statistically unreliable.

★ ★ ★

The closet was a crowded place in the 1980's. Most of us were in and out of it several times a day, depending on where we lived and worked, and with whom. Unlike many people I knew, I could be out at the office, since the public defender's agency was a little island of personal freedom in the ocean of homophobia.

But even at the PD's office, there were different degrees of out-ness. I could be *all* out with queer colleagues, and quietly out with straight ones. I always tried to straighten up a bit around the support staff, who tended to be more conservative. And of course we all snapped the closet door shut behind us at the entrance to the courthouse. A lawyer's sexual orientation could jeopardize their client's case in a court room. Homophobia was alive and well in the Boston courts. Every morning the Second Session judge and court officers would enjoy a few minutes of comic relief at the expense of the trans women held overnight for the crime of being a "Common Nightwalker." Unlike straight women picked up for the same crime, trans women and cross-dressing men were a source of great entertainment for the law-abiding, round-bellied white men in black robes and blue uniforms who laughed and poked fun at them on the record. This was simply the lay of the land, the state of the law.

Court is theatre anyway; everyone dons a costume and puts on a performance. A bit of script, a lot of improv, with lives hanging in the balance. This is nothing new, but the stakes for your client are higher if you let your queer slip show.

The people most shocked by any mention of homophobia were straight liberals, who believed America, or at least Massachusetts, and certainly Boston and Cambridge, had moved lightyears beyond the bad old days of queer-bashing. But in fact, in the 1980's, the police routinely made sweeps of gay hangouts—popular rest areas, parking lots, and phragmites-filled sections of the Fens—and brought criminal charges of Unnatural Acts against the men they hauled in. Twenty years later, even after gay marriage would become legal in Massachusetts, these men (now middle-aged), would still have to register as sex offenders for the rest of their lives, as a result of a twenty-year reach-back provision in the sex offender laws enacted in 1996. My office would fight these newly enacted laws, and would be ostracized for it.

★ ★ ★

After a few weeks I got the impression that Maddie wasn't familiar with queerdom. She seemed to stiffen a bit once when I mentioned my girlfriend in conversation. A momentary deer-in-the-headlights look. But maybe I was wrong; maybe her discomfort had more to do with her beauty. I tried to imagine what it would be like having to walk around looking so stunning all day long. She probably had to fend off people hitting on her constantly. To put her at ease as we talked, I rambled on to another subject. But I could see her turning the information over in her mind; something in her eyes told me that she was still stuck on the realization that I had a *girlfriend*.

Years later, Maddie told me about that first summer we met. After one of the classes, she'd overheard me talking to another classmate. Maddie was shocked to hear me say my girlfriend was a married woman ten years older than me with two children. *I had trouble sleeping that night,* she told me, smiling at the memory. It had never occurred to her that an apparently straight wife and mother (*like her!*) could be so radically attracted to, and involved with, another woman. *It sort of blew my mind,* she said. *It made me question myself.* She started to wonder—had she ever felt attracted to any of her women friends?

★ ★ ★

I first met her husband, Rafi, on the page. He appeared as a character in excerpts of Maddie's novel that she submitted every few weeks in our fiction workshop. She portrayed him as handsome and intense, quick-witted and haunted by the war, about which he did not want to talk. His story immediately piqued my interest.

Rafi had survived the Holocaust as a child in Poland. His father had been killed by the Nazis, and his mother had bleached his hair blond to appear Aryan. The evening we first workshopped Maddie's chapter, I approached her after class.

"My parents have a similar story," I said, "except they're not Jewish." We stood on an asphalt path outside the library. The night was warm, the air feathery on my arms.

I told her the story I'd grown up with: my parents had fallen in love in Poland before the war and were engaged to marry. But when the war broke out, my father was deported to Siberian labor camps for six years. My mother cut her hair short, dressed as an Italian soldier, and marched out of Poland with the Italian army. She was arrested, wound up in an Italian concentration camp, and eventually went to live with her older sister who had married an Italian Count in Rome. Years later, my father escaped from the Gulag, walked across Europe by night as a fugitive, and found my mother in Rome. They married ten years to the day since they first met.

Maddie listened quietly, then tilted her head. "They're Jewish," she said.

Her directness caught me off guard. We barely knew each other.

"No, Catholic," I explained. "The war wreaked havoc on everyone, not just the Jews." This was the line my mother had told me since I was a child. I had no reason to doubt her; after all, she'd lived through the war, I hadn't.

Maddie shook her head slowly. "I don't buy it. Someone in your family had to be Jewish. If your mother was Catholic, why would she have to dress up as an Italian soldier and leave

Poland? She would still have family and friends there. So would your father."

She was quiet for a moment. "Look, I've done a lot of research on Jewish anti-Semitism. And I'm telling you, their story just doesn't make sense unless someone in your family is Jewish."

Her insistence annoyed me. I'd never heard of Jewish anti-Semitism, and the suggestion that my parents were anti-Semitic was absurd. "Why would they lie about it?" I said. "Their best friends are Jews. *And* Holocaust survivors."

She smiled, such neat white teeth. "It's more common than you think. I didn't find out my own mother was Jewish till a few years ago. My father didn't even know he'd married a Jew."

This got my attention. "Was she also a survivor?"

Maddie laughed. "No, she was from New Hampshire. She just wanted to improve her station."

Mosquitos were starting to land. "Where are you headed?" she asked, hoisting her leather messenger bag higher on her shoulder. She offered me a ride and we discovered we were neighbors—my apartment was two blocks from her penthouse on a tree-lined street.

"You should do some research," she said when she dropped me off. "We'll talk."

★ ★ ★

She was right. Everyone in my family turned out to be Jewish. But I wouldn't find that out until years later, when I finally did a ton of research and wrote a book about my parent's survival of the Holocaust. But that is another story altogether.

Back in 1987 I didn't realize that all three of us—Maddie, Rafi, and I—shared a history of hidden identity and passing as mainstream; we were all missing parts of ourselves. The enormity of what I didn't know about my identity back then is breathtaking, considering my lifelong devotion to self-absorption. It would take me years to realize that Maddie essentially introduced me to myself—as if she and Rafi and I were long lost members of the same family.

★ ★ ★

She'd lived in Israel for more than a decade, she told me. I didn't know anyone who had been to Israel. I didn't know that my aunt spent three weeks in Tel Aviv every year visiting her best friend, a fellow Holocaust survivor. I could barely find Israel on a map.

She drove a Jeep through the streets of Boston a decade before anyone considered operating such a vehicle east of the Rockies.

She wore black Spanish leather boots, thin and soft, that came up to her knees; no make-up, and clothes with lots of flow. Balloon pants, coats with yards of fabric, shirts with tails left out. She rolled up the sleeves of her *t-shirts*, turning the most mundane piece of clothing into a fashion statement. She wasn't afraid of belts.

She asked questions about everything. She listened to the answers.

She didn't take herself too seriously. Despite her private school pedigree, international sophistication, and fluency in three languages, she was very down-to-earth.

She missed her father who had just died months earlier. "He was a real sweetie," she said. "You don't find that often."

Her mother, with whom she'd had a much more complicated relationship, had died years before.

Her husband, Rafi, was a Big Deal documentary film producer for public television. Constantly on the go, traveling all over the place, easily bored. "He never stays where he's put," she said.

★ ★ ★

I met him in person later that summer. Stratis, our teacher, threw a party for our writing class and invited us to bring our significant others. I brought no one, because Carla, my girlfriend at the time, was at home eating dinner with her husband and kids. I was almost thirty; Maddie was ten years older, and Rafi was forty-six. My first impression: shock and disappointment. He was old, tired, used-up. He had a big head, burly shoulders, a belly, and he barely reached Maddie's height. Maybe if he stood up straight, he would look better. Maybe if he made an effort. He wore ho-hum slacks and an Oxford shirt straining at the chest, sleeves rolled up to expose those thick hairy arms. His stubble beard filled his face like ground cover, stopping just an inch below his deep-set eyes. I'd read about this handsome, heroic adventurer in Maddie's stories, and he looked nothing like the part. I'd been duped. What did she see in this guy? Ok, yes, he was broad-shoul-dered and powerfully built, blocky as a steam shovel, if you went for that sort of thing. His accent was thick and vaguely famil-iar—a mix of Eastern Europe and the Middle East. But he was nothing like the dazzling man I'd pictured from her writing.

We stood around holding plastic cups of wine, crunching on carrot sticks and cheese cubes, making small talk. After brief introductions, Rafi spent the rest of the hour talking with Stratis. He had quickly sized up the room, and dismissed us as unworthy. Stratis, on the other hand, was a Greek immigrant, poet, novelist, and artist, who had survived both the German occupation and the Greek Civil War as a child. The two of them hit it off.

I didn't see Rafi again until a few weeks later, when I was at their apartment one evening. He hulked through the living room while Maddie and I sat on the couch, going over edits of our stories.

"Where's my wallet?" he asked Maddie.

"Do you remember Helen?" she said, introducing us again. "From the writing class."

He nodded. "My wallet?"

"It's next to your pack."

"Where is that?"

"On the dresser. Right where you left it."

He stalked off.

"Sorry," Maddie said, shaking her head. "He has no manners."

We heard the door to the apartment close behind him.

"He produces films on three continents," she said. "But he can't find his wallet unless someone is there to hand it to him."

★ ★ ★

The class ended, summer was over. Stratis urged Maddie and me to apply to his alma mater, the MFA Program for Writers at Warren Wilson College in Swannanoa, North Carolina. We'd never heard of it before. It sounded like some junior college in a dreamscape, but he explained that it was the first low-residency MFA program; students and faculty convened on campus twice a year for a ten-day residency of classes and workshops, during which each student was assigned to work one-on-one with a faculty supervisor for the next six months, submitting work by mail on a demanding schedule. It would take at least two years and five residencies to complete the program. We eagerly sent away for applications.

CHAPTER 2

I was afraid to ask her; she was afraid to ask me, but it turned out we both got in. Warren Wilson College is about 900 miles south of Boston, on the outskirts of Pisgah National Forest. You take a plane to Charlotte, NC, then switch to a local plane that makes the hop to Asheville, then rent a car and drive half an hour to Swannanoa. Rolling hills, misted forests, farmland. It was early January, 1988, just four months after the Cambridge summer class had ended; Maddie and I left the snowbanks of Boston for the damp browns and blues of western North Carolina.

By then we'd known each other for half a year, but I still felt out of my depths, utterly mesmerized—not only by the contours of her body, but even more by the way her mind worked—the odd angled insights, the sheer range of motion and emotion of her thoughts and words. Maddie seemed to glide along on a cool breeze, while rocking a sharp wit and spiky intellect.

One evening a few months earlier I'd been at her place, discussing "The Death of Ivan Ilyich"—an assignment for a workshop—and she suddenly blurted, "You know what bugs me about Tolstoy?"

Her emerald eyes sparkled, momentarily rendering me speechless.

"His wife," she said. "She was never given any credit as a writer and photographer in her own right."

Maddie, I knew, had been a photographer and photojournalist. She'd once shown me some of her photos—lush black and white images of Bedouins that she'd taken ten years earlier, winning first prize in the "Israel Through the Camera's Eye" competition.

"Tolstoy's wife was a photographer?"

"*And* a writer," Maddie said. "In addition to having his thirteen children."

I didn't know that about Mrs. Tolstoy. "*Wives*," I said, shaking my head, wondering how Maddie felt being married to Rafi, the Great Film Producer. "Notice any similarities?"

She gave me a wry smile. "Best not to compare ourselves to the Russians."

We'd spent hours that fall discussing books and authors we loved, exchanging our own work, and talking about stories we wanted to write. Most of my stories were inspired by my clients' alleged crimes—botched robberies involving gunfire and bite-marks, heroin trafficking in beauty salons, etc. Maddie, on the other hand, was working on her autobiographical novel. By now she had told me much of Rafi's background and her own.

★ ★ ★

She first met him in 1964 at an outdoor volleyball game at Harvard, a social event for foreign students. She'd tagged along with her older sister, Chase. Maddie was still in high school, Rafi was twenty-three. Cue the glorious sunny day, shorts and t-shirts, free love.

"He made a play for Chase almost immediately," Maddie told me. "My sister is …" She tilted her head and smiled a bit archly. "Let's just say that like most guys, he was arrested by her curves." But Chase was with Andy, her math prodigy boyfriend who had gotten his PhD at twenty-two and was already a professor at Harvard at the time. So Rafi settled for the more coltish Maddie. They talked and flirted, held hands. At the end of the day, she let him lead her back to his room.

As Maddie told it, she was surprised she'd attracted the interest of such an exotic creature. The boys she knew were pale and smooth-skinned. Their paths were paved and pre-paid; their futures fully furnished. This man was swarthy, with a rogue's swagger, a thick accent and crinkly eyes when he smiled. She was smitten. "You should do something that scares you every day," she liked to say. At seventeen, she wanted to be an adventurer, the sort of girl who could fuck a sexy man on a whim. So she did.

I was amazed by her boldness. When I was seventeen, I'd been terrified of sex, and dismissed it from my mind altogether. I'd quit high school after my junior year, impatient to get to college—not to begin the adventure of my life, but to impress my parents by burying myself under a pile of books. I could not be bothered with boys at the time.

Back in 1964, after Maddie and Rafi started dating, her mother, Constance, was appalled by her youngest daughter's choice. According to Maddie, her mother had been a brilliant student and social climber; Constance had catapulted herself from humble origins to Harvard University, where she'd snagged a husband with gobs of money—*old* money. ("Of New England founding-fathers stock" the *Globe* Obit put it, when he died in 1986. "The lanky Yankee" he was called by colleagues in his white-shoe law firm and at the State House.) They were among an elite social circle of Boston Brahmins, members of an exclusive club that did not admit Jews or people of color.

Constance immediately began a campaign to get rid of Rafi. She invited him to lunch at The Country Club (as it was casually called), praised his intelligence and good looks, and confided that Maddie was really not very bright—a mediocre student with neither talent nor direction. "You will lose interest in her," Constance assured him. "She's my daughter and I love her, but the fact is, she's rather shallow and insubstantial."

According to Maddie, Rafi was amused by her mother's tactics. He never suspected that Constance, herself, might be Jewish, but he did know that anti-Semitism was responsible for her solicitous efforts. While Maddie was at school, Constance threw luncheon parties at her hacienda-style mansion in Brookline. She invited Rafi to meet her many friends and encouraged him to date their beautiful daughters. At one such event, Constance and her guests were seated at the Spanish dining table overlooking green landscaped lawn, trees, and gardens. The ladies sipped Chablis, nibbled at their shrimp cocktail, and discussed upcoming performances of the Boston Symphony Orchestra or their latest trips to Europe. Seated among the elegantly dressed women, Rafi suddenly interrupted the conversation. "Wait, what is that smell?" he said in mock alarm, sniffing the air. The ladies stopped talking and stared at him. He lifted one arm, dipped his nose to his armpit and inhaled deeply. "Aaaah," he said with a broad smile. "That's it, I smell a Jew!"

Maddie's mother decided to take a more direct approach. She invited Rafi to lunch once again at The Country Club and offered to pay him to leave her daughter alone. He thanked her, ordered dessert, and told her he did not want her money. It was up to her daughter, he said. When he reported her mother's ploy to Maddie, she was furious. It was true, she didn't care that much about her studies. Instead of returning to college her sophomore year, she ran off to Israel to be with him in June, 1967. As it turned out, she arrived in Jerusalem on the eve of the Six-Day War.

At 10:00 the next morning, over 6,000 Jordanian shells hit Jerusalem, damaging nearly a thousand buildings not far from

Rafi's home. For the next several hours, heavy machine and mortar fire rained down on the city.

"I called my parents to let them know where I was, and that I was ok," Maddie said. "They were apoplectic. They had thought I was back at my dorm in college." She shrugged. "My father took it better than my mother."

I said nothing, stunned by Maddie's gutsiness. She'd run off to Israel as a *teenager*, thumbing her nose at her mother. At twenty-nine, I could barely cross state lines to go for a ski weekend without letting my mother know. It wasn't Maddie's travel to a foreign country that impressed me; it was Maddie's defiance of her parents that blew my mind.

With the outbreak of the Six-Day War, Rafi was immediately called back into service, so Maddie found herself spending her first weeks in Israel with his mother, who had been visiting her son that summer. Over time, Maddie learned Hebrew, completed her college degree in Jerusalem, had two children, and lived there for a dozen years as a *shiksa* before finding out—from a first cousin!— that her own mother (and therefore Maddie) was born a Jew.

Maddie was thirty-four when she learned this. She confronted her mother, and Constance grudgingly admitted it was true. "But she'd hidden it from my father," Maddie said. "He didn't even know he'd married a Jew!"

I don't know who finally broke the news to him, but he took it hard. Eventually he told Maddie he was glad he hadn't known Constance was Jewish, because he would never have married her; it would have been out of the question.

★ ★ ★

I was struck by the similarities between her family and mine, even though I still knew very little about my own family in 1987.

It seemed uncanny that Rafi was from *my parents' hometown* of Lvov in eastern Poland, and that both his family and my parents' families had all been killed in the war; that both Rafi and my parents had managed to escape, and eventually emigrated to the States. It also seemed remarkable that my mother's sister had married an Italian Count, leaping from poverty to royalty through marriage, much as Maddie's mother had done.

Of course it was our passion for writing that had brought us together, but Maddie and I shared a deeper bond of complicated family histories. I'd been drawn to Maddie because of her husband's escape from the Nazis, similar to that of my own parents'. And Maddie had been drawn to me because she suspected that like her, I, too, would discover my own hidden Jewish identity. Within months I was beginning to think that Maddie was right—maybe my mother and aunt were Jewish, too. Maybe even my father! I was a bit embarrassed by this fantasy, because it seemed childish to want to be just like my new best friend.

Besides, I thought, my parents were nothing like Maddie's. My parents had been penniless immigrants who had clawed their way into the middle class. They had no use for country clubs. What they did share with Maddie's family was their intellectual elitism—literature, art, classical music and opera were their gods. But socially, my parents and Maddie's were worlds apart.

Even so, I wanted Maddie's hunch about my family to be true. For one thing, Judaism just seemed like a better "fit" for my family than Catholicism. Let's face it: we were lousy Catholics. When I was a kid, my mother told me that Confession was a Catholic practice that had enabled Catholics to commit atrocities throughout history with a clear conscience. That made an impression on me. At the age of six, with my mother's permission (and possibly to her relief), I stopped going to church altogether. All my life I'd gravitated toward survivors—it had nothing to do with religion, it had to do with my gut sense of belonging. It's what had drawn me to Rafi's story in the first place.

I had another reason for wishing my family were Jewish: Keeping a secret of such magnitude could help explain why my family had always been so cosmically fucked-up. Our dysfunction (which we vigilantly kept hidden from the rest of the world) was vast. We'd been in family therapy since I was eight years old, but we only seemed to get worse over time. If my parents were secret Jews—hiding in their own closet for so many decades—no wonder we were nuts. It would just *make sense.*

* * *

In those days, despite my efforts to appear self-sufficient—a competent attorney and responsible adult—I was plagued by an insatiable existential *neediness.* I tried very hard to hide my hunger from the world. I used to wait till I was alone at home before tearing into boxes of cookies and ice cream—poor substitutes for love, I knew, but more available on demand than people. I tried not to think about the self-destruction that lay at the heart of all hunger denied. Every morning, I swam a mile to dissolve my food transgressions in chlorinated water.

This lurching back and forth from food to exercise formed the drumbeat to my days, a steady distraction from the fact that I really had no idea who I was or what I wanted.

CHAPTER 3

January, 1988

Our prop plane touched down at the tiny Asheville airport, taxied to a stop, and Maddie and I climbed down the stairs to the tarmac. We'd been talking about the story I'd submitted for the Warren Wilson workshop—"Mudsongs," inspired by my stint as a Peace Corps Volunteer four years earlier in a remote mountain village of Lesotho. The story itself was pure fiction, told in the first person by a young Basotho girl—just one of my clueless forays into cultural appropriation. (Years later, I would be gently told by my thesis advisor to put the story in a drawer; lock the drawer; throw away the key.)

I was now anxiously anticipating the cold-blooded massacre of the story in workshop, while Maddie was worried about her own submitted chapter—an early scene in her courtship, when teenaged Maddie asked Rafi what the Jews had done to provoke the Holocaust.

"The worst part about it is that it's true," she said, as I got behind the wheel of our boxy Ford rental car. "I really asked him that."

"No way."

"I'd never heard of the Holocaust! They didn't teach it at Beaver Country Day."

I couldn't decide what was more ludicrous—failing to teach the Holocaust or naming a private girl's school *Beaver Country Day*. "Seriously?"

"For real! We didn't mix with Jews, much less talk about the Holocaust."

"So how did Rafi respond?"

She groaned. "Let's just say I got educated." The rest of her chapter, she said, was fiction. Well, some was fiction, some was true. "I think fiction is more true than reality," she said as we exited the highway, following the typed directions we'd been sent. I felt like we were on an adventure together, a sort of treasure hunt.

We drove east to Swannanoa, asking all the big questions: What is truth? What is fictional truth? What is the writer's responsibility? Could language ever capture the precise quality of experienced reality, given the inevitable distortions of memory? And what about the betrayals of unconscious biases, the imprecision of words themselves, the idiosyncrasies of syntax, even grammar?

"Ok," I said, "so we can agree it's impossible to write the truth about anything."

She smiled mischievously. "That's one way of looking at it. The other way is that everything is true, in some way or another. When you write a story, the truth of who you are is revealed on the page, no matter how you try to hide it."

Maybe that was true of identity, too. No matter how much I'd tried to be straight, I was queer. And no matter how much my parents pretended to be Catholic, it turns out they were not.

★ ★ ★

Just two months earlier, I had broken up with my married girlfriend Carla—not because I'd grown tired of her, but because

I was sideswiped by the sudden realization that *I wanted her too much*. She and I had returned from a week's vacation in Puerto Rico in November, when to my horror, I burst into tears at Logan airport. It dawned on me that we were *parting*—she was going home to her husband and kids on their straight-laced suburban street, while I was returning to my empty apartment in the city.

The problem was not Carla's husband—he'd agreed to let her date women, as long as she told no one, including their children. I was not Carla's first girlfriend. When I'd picked her up from their house the week before, her husband had shaken my hand warmly, wished us both a wonderful trip, and promised to take care of the kids in our absence. The kids, still in grade school, waved goodbye, thinking nothing of it. They seemed fine. No, the problem was *me*.

"I can't bear to leave you," I blubbered, as we got into my car at the Logan parking lot. It was late at night; the streets were empty as I drove her home past the dark houses and tidy lawns of her neighborhood, tears streaming down my cheeks. She spoke gently, as if to a young child, assuring me that nothing had changed; we would see each other the following weekend. When we turned onto her street, she withdrew her hand from mine, straightened up, and leaned away from me. "We can't do this here," she said quietly. "Someone might see." A state trooper lived in the house across from hers. His empty cruiser was parked in his driveway. She slipped out of the car without touching me.

I drove home. Shame didn't begin to capture it. I was gutted, crushed to find myself so needy, so desperate for complete immersion in the monumental mindfuck of love. How could I have made such a colossal miscalculation? I'd gone from wanting someone who would place no demands on me to wanting something closer to Total Fusion.

I called her the next day in a well of humiliation and tears, apologized, and told her I couldn't see her anymore. I refused even to meet, knowing I could not resist the urge to fall into her arms again. I was appalled by my cowardice. And I felt like a fool. After all, I'd entered into this relationship with my eyes wide open, knowing full well there was a giant trap door in the middle, yet I still managed to fall right through it. There was nothing to discuss. I was an idiot, having imagined the rules of gravity did not apply to me.

I was too ashamed to mention any of this to Maddie. At some point that winter, I told her that Carla and I were no longer together, but I didn't elaborate and she didn't ask.

★ ★ ★

The ten-day Warren Wilson residency kicked off that afternoon with an informal reception for faculty and students— maybe fifty of us in all, ranging from late-twenties to mid-sixties. Maddie and I liked the shaggy dog feel of the place: two fold-out tables with bowls of potato chips, 20-ounce bottles of Pepsi and Dr. Pepper, cheap wine, plastic cups. Cans of beer sweated in a steel tub of liquefying ice.

"Sort of like Cannes?" I asked. She'd told me that every spring Rafi was invited to the Cannes Film Festival, as one of the perks of his job as a film producer. Maddie hated the gala parties that he loved so much; he always begged her to go with him, to schmooze with movie stars and other celebrities in tuxedos and gowns. Maddie considered it a form of torture.

She and I had discussed our game plan in advance. We split up and talked to as many people as we could, having read almost everyone's work in advance; later that night, after the fiction and poetry readings, we got together and compared notes. The students and faculty had come from all over the country; a few had even come from overseas. Back in their civilian lives, our fellow students were doctors and ranchers and waitresses and lawyers and bartenders and artists and professors and musicians and dogwalkers and scientists and bankers and temps—all of us suffering from a passion for writing that was not yet fully requited.

Classes began first thing in the morning, and for the next ten days, we followed an insane schedule: wall-to-wall lectures, classes, workshops, individual faculty-student meetings, and after-dinner readings that ran till late at night. Maddie and I went to classes together, but we were assigned different workshops, so afterwards we'd debrief before racing off to the next lecture. For ten days we discussed the shapes and sounds of sentences, the missed opportunities of the close third person versus omniscient point of view; the search for *duende* in poetry and prose. Characters from stories by Babel and Chekhov and O'Connor were mentioned in workshops as if we'd all just had coffee with them before class.

It seemed so incongruous that in this sleepy backwater of Swannanoa, such an electric fire of literary minds was ablaze. No one slept more than a few hours a night. Conversations lasted into the wee hours, and then we all had a ton of work to do, hundreds of pages to read, stories to plunder for classes and workshops each day, and personal crises of existential self-doubt to grapple with.

Maddie and I had come to the residency as good friends; by the end, we felt we'd known each other for years. We flew home together, utterly spent after our ten-day literary orgy. Returning from Warren Wilson with her was completely different from returning from Puerto Rico with Carla two months earlier: for one thing, Maddie and I were not lovers. (At the time, the very idea that we might become lovers was inconceivable. She was straight as an arrow and categorically out of my league.) And since Maddie and I lived so close to each other, we simply hopped into a cab to her place, split the fare, then I rolled my suitcase the two blocks to my apartment. Parting was a cinch.

We vibrated for weeks afterwards, still giddy from the overdose of self-exposure as writers, even as we returned to our daily life and responsibilities. Our semester's reading and writing assignments were all-consuming, so now I squeezed my day job into my writing life. Fortunately I loved my PD job and adored my boss. Anita was a drop-dead gorgeous African American woman with a short Afro, a brilliant mind, and a killer sense of humor. She overflowed with juice. It was impossible not to be swept off your feet in her presence—she commanded a room. In fact, she commanded the entire building, and when she walked down the hall in her bright-colored blouses, slim skirts, and black stockings, heads turned. In an office of mostly white men in those days, she stood out as a splash of exquisite color and creative energy; she would later become the first woman (and the first African American) to lead the agency, before accepting a Senate-confirmed Presidential appointment in Clinton's Justice Department.

She wore chunky faux-gold clip-on earrings and, like everything else she did, she wielded them with balletic grace. Whenever the phone rang (constantly), she made a ninja-quick move with her hands. As one hand reached for the phone, the other shot across her chest and up to her face, plucking the earring at the precise moment that the phone arrived at her ear, and she began to talk. She had perfected this move through years of answering phones, and her hands moved automatically, even on those rare occasions when there was no earring to remove.

The year before, Anita had selected me as her side-kick, saving me from my thrilling but self-annihilating stint as a trial attorney in the agency. (I had barely lasted a year as a trial lawyer, a job I loved, but that had left me with zero time to sleep, see friends, or do anything else. I was in court five days a week, at the jails on nights and weekends, and crime scenes around the clock.) Now that I was a petit bureaucrat, I finally had the time and bandwidth to return to writing after years of neglect.

As state employees, our jobs were typically insane: Anita and I oversaw the work of about three thousand private attorneys, mostly solo practitioners, throughout the state. They were assigned hundreds of thousands of indigent cases each year—mostly criminal cases, but also child welfare, termination of parental rights, mental health commitments, etc.

We had a big tent and no staff. Our days were filled with surprises. Anita created a statewide legal services system out of nothing, and took me along. I had no talent for that sort of vision, but I was good at riding shotgun with her. I liked doing whatever Anita dreamt up for me to do; usually this involved drafting legal service procedures, attorney performance standards, and oversight proposals. It also involved investigating attorney fuckups, and protecting clients from attorneys who had gone off the rails. Busy, busy, busy.

Anita's work ethic jibed with mine. She was on fire with ideas and strategic schemes—she would charge in and crank out projects around the clock. And then she would goof off. She didn't care about nine-to-five, she cared about results. She also didn't want to know the details if you needed time off.

In the beginning I used to call to explain why, for example, I couldn't be in the office till noon one day. "Don't," she'd interrupt me mid-sentence. "I don't care. Just tell me when you'll be here."

"Noon."

"That's all you need to say," she'd instruct. "Never tell anyone your business. See you then."

★ ★ ★

While I was at work, Maddie looked after her kids and held down the household. She had quit her job as a photographer for Polymorph Films, in order to focus on her writing. Every two weeks we met in Cambridge with our writing group. I would take the T from work, and Maddie drove me home afterwards, and we'd make plans to get together over the weekend. Whenever I went over to their place, Rafi was usually away.

Their kids were eight and ten, doing a million things. Rachel, the older one, sailed, danced, debated, went out with friends. Eva was quieter, more studious, and a budding gymnast. I tagged along when Maddie dropped her off at gymnastics one day; then she took me shopping. She tried to elevate my look. I didn't have a look. I didn't care about clothes, or at least I didn't care about fashion. My top priority was comfort. Clothing had to be roomy, non-binding, rugged, and unfussy. Ditto shoes, only more so. Forget heels, platforms, strappy things.

While Maddie tried to upgrade my appearance that spring, my queer friends applied themselves to the equally hopeless task of trying to get me back in the dating game. They invited me over for a party, gathered all their friends, and waited for things to click. But I was never much of a partier to begin with, and this was the usual incestuous local lesbian scene. The gay community in Boston was so small back then, everyone had already fallen in love with one another, moved in together, broken up, become best friends; then fallen in love with their ex-lovers' former lovers, etc. The whole spin cycle depressed me.

Another friend dragged me along on a hike to Lonesome Lake in the White Mountains with a group that called themselves the Boston Professional Women. I bristled at the term—a social group of lesbians who obviously wanted to distinguish themselves from sleazy pool-room dykes with bad attitudes and matching teeth. This annoyed me on principle, but my friend assured me they had no standards; everyone was welcome.

It was a hot, hazy summer day, perfect for the blackflies and mosquitoes that resided in the swamps surrounding Lonesome Lake, where the crowds of day hikers were a sure thing. I hated Lonesome Lake for all of these reasons, and I hated it because it was an easy hike (I was an insufferable mountain snob in those days), and I hated it because I preferred to hike alone, and I hated myself for being such a social chicken.

All nineteen of us Professional Woman clomped up that gentle trail, each in our overkill steel-shank boots with Vibram lug soles. When we got back to Boston that evening I thanked my friend for her efforts, but I doubted I would find a girlfriend this way.

Besides, who had time to date? I was swamped with work at the office, and swamped with deadlines for the writing program—a packet due every three weeks. For each packet you had to write a new story, a revised story, three essays on three books assigned in advance, and a long letter outlining your writing process, baring your soul, and asking questions. You mailed all of this with a self-stamped return envelope to your faculty supervisor, then got cracking on the next packet, while biting your nails in anticipation of your supervisor's response. This was where my passion and courage went in those days; I had none left to meet anyone. Besides, Maddie and I were spending more and more time together, growing closer in this intensive boot camp for baby writers.

★ ★ ★

At last our six-month semester ended, and Maddie and I went back for our second residency in July. I had an entire new look this time, created by Maddie: pale yellow Fruit of the Loom t-shirt (with sleeves rolled twice, setting them at an angle), a pair of black cuffed Poco Loco shorts; black Spanish boots to match Maddie's (which cost a fortune—over $200; I'd never spent that much on footwear, except my ski mountaineering boots.) And a scarf—I'm pretty sure she tried to get me to wear scarves. I wore one on the first day, shocking the entire group. I still had my Dartmouth Outward Bound t-shirt (forest green, with the emblem of the compass surrounded by the motto "To serve, to strive, and not to yield,") that I wore on runs through the woods. And my junky t-shirts and shorts that I used for loungewear. But Maddie had taken me on as a project: turning me from an eight-year-old boy into a woman with some zing. I was game, as long as it was Maddie. I liked her attention. I liked her assessment of my body in clothes. "You need bright jewel colors," she said. *Jewel colors?* She wanted me in turquoise, topaz, colors that popped. I complied. I enjoyed the pleasure she took in me, but the clothes? Who cared, I'd never liked dressing up. I'd dedicated my life to dressing *down*. But this was a way to let Maddie play with me, to outfit me as someone partly true, and partly new. It was an intimate game of make-believe, a fiction. And like all fiction, an essential truth lay at the heart of it. It was a way of being together.

CHAPTER 4

You have to come out in the boat, she said. It was late July, 1988, a few weeks after our second residency, when we went for an afternoon sail—just Rafi, Maddie, me, and the kids.

I hadn't been sailing since I was nine at a summer camp in Maine, in a little sunfish the size of a bumper car—one kid per boat—that we steered around clumps of kelp in the Penobscot Bay. Sailing was ok; I could take it or leave it. But now I wanted to go sailing with Maddie and Rafi for what it signified—proof (in my mind) that I had entered their inner circle, that I was now a bona fide friend, of which I assumed they had hundreds.

As Rafi steered us out of the marina, you could see in his razor-blade eyes the intensity of his concentration. Above the massif of his shoulders, his head seemed to turn on a swivel, scanning the horizon, checking the sails, calculating currents, wind, angle of the sun, boat speed, the slightest shifts in movement. It was like alpine skiing, I thought, in which every cell in your body is focused on the terrain and the turn of your edges as you fly across moguls, patches of ice or pockets of powder. He was skiing on the water in a 50-foot, 5-ton boat rather than a pair of 10-pound skis but the combination of intense focus and wild freedom was the same.

Rafi had fallen in love with sailing as a boy, when he'd arrived in Israel after the war. He built his first sailboat at the age of twelve and launched it in the Mediterranean. By the time I met him, he'd spent over three decades skippering sailboats in

Israel, along the coast of New England, in the Mediterranean and Caribbean. He had taught Maddie and the girls to sail, and they spent family vacations on the boat.

Now he was hopping from one narrow surface to the other, surprisingly agile for a man his size, yanking ropes, untying and re-tying knots. Maddie assisted with such fluidity, it was clear they had become a sailing unit. And the girls, already seasoned sailors at nine and eleven, knew exactly what to do when their father called out commands. I was relegated the role of barnacle, my sole job to gaze out to sea and repose.

It was hot and muggy when we set out, but soon we were cutting across the chop, the air gauzy, cooled by a breeze from the Northeast. I was glad they'd told me to bring a sweater. Maddie left Rafi to manage for himself once we were out on the open ocean, and the girls took over as his crew.

"Brace about!" he shouted. "Brace *about*!"

I heard it as "Race about," which is what the girls did, running and yanking on ropes to turn the sail.

"Let go the sheets and braces!" Rafi called. "Make all!"

We meandered around the Boston Harbor Islands, and Maddie settled in next to me at the stern, well out of earshot from the others. She told me that she didn't mind sailing anymore; she actually had come to enjoy it, although it still grated on her nerves that she (like all wives, she said) was always the crew and never the captain. It was a male-dominated enterprise. Wherever they sailed—whether in the Caribbean or the Mediterranean or around New England—it was always the same: the man skippered, and the woman followed his orders. "And Rafi's not always a friendly Captain," Maddie added. "He barks commands and expects immediate execution. He has no patience for a moment's delay." It had taken Maddie years to learn the ropes (literally) and to understand Rafi's interpretation of the ocean and how to maneuver across it.

"It's an enormous amount of work," she said. "And it smacks of the whole male power thing in marriage."

I knew I could never do it. I wasn't even being ordered around, and I still found it jarring. Maddie, I thought, seemed to have settled into the role of well-mannered rebel. She was tolerant and even-tempered, even when she raised objections. Unlike Rafi, who growled and bellowed and stormed out of rooms, when Maddie got angry, she knit her brow and sighed with exasperation. She almost never raised her voice or said anything ugly.

★ ★ ★

A few weeks earlier, when Maddie and I were up on her roof deck, she and the kids told me about the worst time she'd ever lost her temper. We were lounging in the sun on her weather-beaten deck chairs, feeling lazy; Rafi was out, as usual. The Hancock Tower, a vertical rectangle of blue-mirrored windows, rose above Back Bay three miles to our east; looking south, you could almost see as far as the Blue Hills Reservation. Every so often Maddie got up to dead-head the gangly array of flowers in giant pots around the deck. Even from across the roof, I marveled at the pirouette of her hands as she plucked the dried blooms. In jeans and t-shirt she seemed to glide across the deck before settling back into her chair.

The kids came up and plopped down on deck chairs next to us. Soon Rachel grew restless and started playing with Maddie's hair—tugging at it and twisting it into little strands. "Really?" Maddie said.

"What?" Rachel smirked. She had Rafi's cocky sense of humor.

"Don't you have something better to do?"

"Oh, am I *bothering* you?" Rachel said, laughing.

Maddie sighed.

"Tell Helen about the time you got really, really mad at us," Rachel said.

"At *you*," Eva corrected.

"*The Time Mummy Blew Up*," Rachel said, turning to me. "It was a couple of years ago."

I liked being included in the kids' banter. It made me feel like part of the family.

"Oh I remember," Maddie said. "You—" she pointed at Rachel, "were being particularly bratty that day."

Rafi had been out of town once again, Maddie explained. She was tired and annoyed at having to cover on short notice. "He never let me know when he was leaving. He would sometimes call from the office in the middle of the day. *Oh I forgot to tell you—I have to be in Washington tonight.* When had he first found out? *It just came up*, he'd say. Later I'd find out it had been planned weeks in advance." Maddie shook her head. "It was the same argument over and over. *Give me some notice*, I'd tell him. *I have to know your schedule. I have to be able to plan around it.*"

"It's a common theme," Rachel said, turning to me.

So here was another one of those days when Maddie found herself alone with the kids for the zillionth time, and the kids, too, reacted to Rafi's abrupt disappearances by acting out. "No one was more obnoxious than me," Rachel said proudly. She quarreled with her sister, talked back to her mother, and stomped around the house.

"Finally Mummy couldn't take it anymore," Rachel said. "She turned to me and shouted, 'Your *attitude*, young lady ...'" Rachel paused, looking from Eva to Maddie. "We both froze," she continued. "We were so shocked that Mummy had raised her voice. Then she finally spat out the word she was looking for: '... *Sucks!*'"

Eva chimed in: "We just stood there and stared at each another. No one knew what to say–"

"We finally burst out laughing," Rachel said.

That was it, the one time Mummy lost her shit and yelled at the kids.

Wow, I thought. Things weren't like that in my family. When we blew up, it could be years before the pieces were even found.

* * *

The wind picked up as Rafi steered us back to the marina. We hopped onto the dock and tied the boat down. It had been a lovely afternoon, mainly because I had felt so privileged to be included in their family outing. I had always wanted this, a family to adopt me, and here I was, allowed in. Not by Rafi particularly—he and I may have exchanged half a dozen words all day. He'd been busy, actively sailing this boat with us in it; to him, I was a piece of luggage.

* * *

Like me, Rafi had grown up knowing very little of his own past. Maddie told me his story one day when we were up on the roof deck again, watering the flowers and herbs. She was an indifferent gardener; the plants that survived had learned to be patient. "When I met him, all he knew was that his father had been killed in the war. His mother never told him anything else."

That sounded familiar. My parents had refused to talk to my sister and me about the war. Their past filled our lives like a dark shadow—menacing but free of details.

When the Six-Day War broke out, Rafi was called back into the army, leaving Maddie alone with his mother, Zevka.

She began recounting her own wartime stories to her son's new teenage American girlfriend. "She would talk to me for hours," Maddie said. "Now that Rafi was away, she told me things she'd never told anyone before. She said she wanted Rafi to know, but she couldn't tell him herself."

So Rafi learned his own story from Maddie. "Telling him about his childhood—I'd never felt that kind of responsibility before," she said. "Like I was the bridge connecting him to his own mother. And to his history."

Rafi's father had owned a factory in Lvov, Maddie told me, the city where my parents were from. But unlike my family who lived in the poor section of town, his were people of means. Rafi was born in July, 1941, weeks after the Nazis invaded and occupied the city. His father, an influential Jewish business leader, was an outspoken critic of the Nazi regime. Within a year or so, these distinctions earned him arrest and imprisonment in the Lublin Castle, about 100 miles northwest of Lvov. He was to be executed by firing squad a few days later.

In a desperate attempt to save her husband, Rafi's mother obtained false papers for herself, her baby, and her husband, assuming the identity of Polish Catholics. She bleached Rafi's hair blond with peroxide, and traveled to Lublin. Her plan, Maddie told me, was to go to the prison with her baby and explain that the Nazis had made a mistake; her husband was not a Jew, but in fact Polish Catholic; she had the papers to prove that the whole family was Catholic. She was young and passionate; without her husband, she didn't care to live.

Friends tried to dissuade her. *It's too risky*, they warned. *The Germans will not believe you, they'll arrest you and kill all three of you. You can't save your husband, but you may still be able to save your son. You have to think of the child.*

But Zevka knew she would never forgive herself if she didn't try to save her husband. What would be the point of her life otherwise? She packed up Rafi and the false papers and traveled to Lublin. She awoke early, Maddie said, and walked to the prison in darkness, the baby in her arms. With each step, she agonized over her decision. She knew it was a long shot. Should she turn back for the baby's sake? But how could she possibly live with herself if she didn't try to save her husband?

At the last minute, she collapsed in tears by the side of the road, and realized that she could not risk her baby's life for her husband's. Her decision would plague her for the rest of her life, Maddie told me. It made for a complicated mother-son relationship. Rafi would be a permanent reminder to her of her betrayal of the man she loved, the reason her husband had been killed while she survived.

It made sense to me that Zevka could not bring herself to tell her son this story, that she would confide instead in his girlfriend—someone who loved Rafi, but who was at a safe remove from the war. I was struck not only by the horror of the story, but also by its familiarity. I had heard similar accounts from survivor friends of my parents, and from books that my mother pressed upon me to read when I was in junior high. My parents wanted me to know about the atrocities of the war; they just couldn't talk to me about it themselves.

Zevka and her baby weathered the remaining years of the war on false papers, moving frequently to keep one step ahead of suspicious neighbors who were eager to turn in Jews for the bounty offered by the Nazis. (This, too, was how my mother had survived, although I wouldn't learn my own mother's story until years later.) Rafi's first languages were Polish and German; his first memory was the stinging of his scalp when his mother regularly bleached his hair with peroxide. The rest of his family was killed. After the war, Rafi and his mother moved to Paris. Zevka was a talented artist, but Maddie didn't say how she managed to support herself and her son over the years. They emigrated to

Israel in 1949, when Rafi was eight. He learned Hebrew, went to school, fell in love with sailing and the sea, and settled into his new life.

But Zevka was unhappy in Israel; in 1956 she moved back to Paris where she would live for most of her life. Rafi, at fifteen, didn't want to leave. He was taken in by his closest friend's family and completed high school in Tel Aviv, then served in the Israeli Army. He came to the States for college, enrolled in Boston University and studied Communications, a field in which he could shape what he saw of the world into stories.

* * *

Not long after I spent the day on the boat with Maddie and Rafi that summer of 1988, a college friend invited me to visit her in New York for the weekend. She knew I was single, and wanted me to meet a friend of hers who had just been dumped. We went to a gay bar and waited for Tori to arrive.

The bar was huge and industrial, a curated frenzy of noise-music. Neon strobe lights made everyone look jumpy. Meeting under such circumstances ensured that we could neither see nor hear one another well, which probably worked to my advantage. Tori turned out to be a hard-bodied little spitfire with an insurrection of wild curly hair exploding in all directions. She told me she was Jewish, a book slut, and had dropped out of Barnard after one year because it wasn't worth the money. She now managed a printing press and made *boo-koo bucks*. I liked her. She was brash, funny and outspoken.

We dated for a few months; she came to visit me in Boston a couple of times, and we got together in Connecticut once for a weekend hike. She was the second woman I'd ever slept with, and I was terribly disappointed. Sex was quick and business-like; she might as well have been a guy, I thought. In December, we went to a gala women's concert at Carnegie Hall, followed by a huge party at the Waldorf. It was a blast to be in such traditional storied spaces with hundreds of other lesbians and queers in all manner of attire: lavender tuxes, peacock-feathered outfits, rainbow-striped hair. But I was a bit unnerved to find that our concert seats were right next to Tori's ex and her new girlfriend. These women were huge, twice our size, and spilled over their seats into ours. I asked them about their work, and tried to pretend everything was fine. The tension among them crackled.

After the party, Tori drove me to her house in New Jersey where I discovered the situation was more complicated than I'd thought. She and her girlfriend owned the house and had been living together for over a decade; they still slept together from time to time. They dated other women and brought them home, apparently to rub each other's noses in their infidelity. The whole thing was just too messy and catty and complicated. I told Tori I didn't think I could be involved in it, and she shrugged and said she understood. We parted ways with ease, neither of our hearts the least bit implicated, much less hurt.

Women, I thought, as I took the train back to Boston. *What the hell?*

I never mentioned my dating adventures to Maddie and she never asked. We mostly talked about writing in those days. Every two weeks we got together with our Cambridge writing group, and on weekends we ran around the Brookline Reservoir together. I'd always sensed that she, like most of my straight friends in those days, was a little uncomfortable with my being queer. It wasn't that my friends were homophobic; they just struck me as awkward and a bit embarrassed around the topic. To avoid saying something clumsy, they said nothing. So I never mentioned anything about my queer life with my straight friends. Our worlds were politely segregated by unspoken agreement.

CHAPTER 5

In January, 1989, Maddie and I flew down to Swannanoa for our third residency. We'd been in the writing program for a year already. One day toward the end of the residency, she pulled me aside. *I need to talk to you. Let's go for a run.*

We looked at the schedule and found a window before dinner. We quickly changed into running clothes and took off into the hills before walking the last few miles back to campus.

"How did you know you were gay?" she said, once we'd slowed to a walk. Her question surprised me; it was a topic we'd both avoided ever since we'd first met a year and a half earlier.

I laughed nervously. "Well it took forever." I was still embarrassed to remember how clueless I'd been. When I'd come out to my lesbian friends six or seven years ago, they'd laughed and patted me on the back. "Congratulations," they said. "We wondered when you'd finally figure it out!"

Maddie's eyes narrowed. "So how did you know? Were you in love with someone?"

"No, that's the crazy thing. I wasn't even *with* anyone when I came out. I had to use the retrospectoscope." I told Maddie that I'd been in therapy when I realized I'd been serially head-over-heels in love with three of my best friends in college, year after year. And even after I figured *that* out, it had taken me another couple of years to act on it. I just had some huge block that prevented me from seeing the obvious.

Our trail brought us to a dirt road, and we followed it down to the valley. The sky loomed gunmetal gray, the air chilly.

"What about ... you know, physically?" she said.

I shook my head. "Well, I had a couple of serious boyfriends, but I assumed I just wasn't that into sex. I mean, sex was ok in limited doses, but mostly I just put up with it."

My mother had once told me that it was the same for her. She had come to visit me during my first year of law school when I was twenty-one, and we stayed up late one night. "Men have the sex drive," she'd said. "Women, not so much."

"So when I finally slept with a woman," I told Maddie, "it flat-out blew my mind. Like, E=mc2 flashed across the sky in neon lights. I was just not prepared for that. I had no idea."

Maddie was quiet for a moment. Our sneakers crunched on the wet dirt. A woodpecker hammered in the distance.

I was uncomfortable with the whole topic of sex—it made me feel stupid and inexperienced. At thirty-one, with my low sexual IQ, I was the last person who should be offering my history to a hetero. I'd always liked sharing coming out stories with fellow queers—it gave us a sense of solidarity, bonding. But talking about my coming out experience with a straight person made me feel like an alien. It only seemed to accentuate our differences.

"I think I was in love with my best friend in Jerusalem," Maddie said, taking me by surprise. "She was older than me by ten years—sort of like you and me." she smiled. "But we were closer than anyone I'd ever known before." Overhead a hawk glided by, soundlessly dismissing us. "Her name is Naomi. We were inseparable. She was married too, with kids, but now I realize—I mean, I'm starting to think—I was more in love with her than with Rafi ... or really, with anyone."

Uh-oh, I thought. This was exactly the kind of thing that gave lesbians a bad rap. *Innocent straight housewife hangs out with known lesbian and is converted to sexual deviancy through predatory subconscious techniques.*

I made an effort to be nonpartisan. "Well, the fact that you and she had a really profound relationship," I said reasonably, "doesn't necessarily mean you're gay. It's possible you just loved someone who happens to be a woman. I don't think you have to worry that it means you're a lesbian."

She frowned and stared at her feet as we walked. I stared at her feet. We had bought matching pink sneakers before coming here.

"Yeah, I'm pretty sure I was in love with Naomi." Her voice trailed off.

Perspiration trickled down the back of my neck. As Maddie's only lesbian friend, I would be the prime suspect for luring her down the evil path of homosexuality. I felt obliged to talk her out of it—whatever she was saying—to protect myself from any accusation of undue influence. "Women just tend to be more affectionate," I said. "They hug each other, they're more demonstrative. It doesn't mean they're gay."

In fact, ever since I'd met Maddie a year and a half earlier, I'd been super careful *never* to touch her. We never hugged hello or goodbye; I'd never offered her so much as a comforting hand on her shoulder, lest she misconstrue it as any kind of advance.

"No, this wasn't like that," Maddie murmured. "This was—I was really *in love* with her."

I became more intrigued, less self-conscious. "So did you ever talk with her about it?"

Maddie shook her head. "No, it never occurred to me. I mean, I didn't think of it like that."

The trees lined up like soldiers along the side of the road, listening.

"So why do you think of it now?"

She stopped and looked at me. Her brow was furrowed, like a child working out a problem. Our eyes met, and she seemed to be looking to me for something—some kind of reassurance or explanation.

"How did she feel about you?" I asked.

"She loved me," she said simply. "We were completely in sync. She knew what I was thinking before I even said a word. She just *got* me. And I felt the same about her."

She started walking again. "But we never talked about our relationship," she said. "We were always ... It never ... " She leaned forward and gathered her hair back in a ponytail. Such an elegant gesture, so smooth and lithe. "When I left Israel," she said, "I missed her so much, it was like a pain in my chest. I couldn't breathe."

This was starting to sound like me when I'd parted from women I'd been in love with in college. When my best friend transferred to Berkeley after our freshman year, I'd cried for months, unable to figure out what was wrong with me. The following year, I fell for a senior, and when she graduated, I was so devastated I went on exchange to Dartmouth for a semester, unable to face living on campus without her. My feelings made no sense to me; I feared I might be slipping into mental illness, a territory my sister had always occupied when we were kids. At least by the time I had my meltdown over leaving Carla, I knew what was going on.

Perhaps Maddie was now beginning to understand that she, too, felt something for Naomi that had never made sense to her before.

"Do you keep in touch with her?" I asked.

"Oh yes," she said. "We've always been in touch. We write, we talk by phone. But she's so busy, you know. We both are. She's a doctor, her husband is a scientist, and their kids are teenagers already. We haven't seen each other in years. It's just … strange."

My discomfort returned as I thought of another classic lesbian trope: *Straight woman becomes enthralled with lesbian friend and wants to "experiment;" lesbian falls hard for her; straight woman breaks lesbian's heart and goes back to men.*

"Well," I said, "did you feel any attraction to her? You know, physically, sexually?"

"I don't know," she said. "I wasn't thinking like that. Or … I don't know what I felt. Maybe I did. I don't know."

Through a break in the woods we could see the faint outline of mountains in the distance, a pale blue line hovering in the sky. "Does it matter?" I asked. "I mean, your relationship with Naomi was—and *is*—whatever it is. You don't have to label or define it. It just is."

She shook her head. "I know, but it *does* matter. Maybe it shouldn't, but it does."

I felt a queasy sense of recognition. We were more alike than I'd thought. Through Maddie, I'd come to suspect my parents were Jewish. And through me, Maddie now recognized her passion for Naomi. We were lightning rods to discover each other's hidden identities.

I didn't think Maddie was queer, but I knew lesbians whom I would *never* have guessed were queer. Besides, did you have to be queer, *per se*, to fall in love with someone of the same sex?

We came to a narrow paved road. "Oh, I know where we are!" I said with relief. "We've still got a ways to go." I looked at my watch. "We're going to miss dinner."

She didn't seem to hear me. "Naomi knew me so well," she said. "I could tell her anything, everything. She knew all about

Rafi, about all the women he fucked, all the affairs he had, all the crap we went through."

I stayed quiet. She'd never mentioned this aspect of her relationship with Rafi—not in our conversations and not in her writing. She'd talked and written about him as a workaholic, an adventurous, gruff, impatient, funny, charismatic, and often insensitive guy, but nothing of his infidelity. I tried not to reveal my shock. Why did I always assume straight people led uncomplicated lives?

She sighed. "Maybe we should run for a bit," she said. We picked up the pace and reached campus after dark. We'd missed dinner, but we had just enough time to shower, change, and make it to the evening readings.

★ ★ ★

The next day was sunny and mild. It was almost the end of the residency, and it showed: everyone had already cycled through all their clothes, and were wearing the same things they'd worn at the beginning. We were all sleep-deprived. No one seemed to bother much with their hair or appearance anymore. We were a tribe of writers closing in on the last leg of our bi-annual vision quest.

Breakfast in the cafeteria: Maddie and I sat across from each other as usual, sucking down coffee. "Did you sleep?" she asked.

I shook my head. "You?"

She laughed. "I was up till three, prepping for class. I got in a few hours."

"What do you have to do today?"

We checked the schedule.

"Let's blow off the 1:00 lecture," she said. "*Lyric Poetry and the Problem of Time*. I didn't make it through the materials."

This is what happened by the eighth or ninth day of the residency. Things fell apart.

"Ok," I said. I hadn't read the materials either.

We agreed to meet in the cafeteria after our morning classes and workshops, make a sandwich, and head out to the hills for a picnic.

The sun had grown lazy by noon, muscled out by clouds. We hiked past the college's pig farm and settled on a patch of grass under a live oak. The mountains looked gentle and friendly in the distance.

"I'm thinking of leaving Rafi," she said.

★ ★ ★

By now, our third residency, I'd gotten to know Rafi as much as I cared to. Bottom line, I thought he was a jerk: arrogant, overbearing, pugnacious. I couldn't imagine what Maddie saw in him, and I'm sure he felt the same about me, if he bothered to think about me at all. Once when I was at their house he'd baited me by making fun of my work representing the indigent. "You know they're all guilty," he said. *Dayr awl gheelty*, it sounded in his thick accent. "They should get a job." *Gitta chub*. I was used to hearing this from otherwise thoughtful people, and tried to talk about broader principles—justice, equality, constitutional rights—but he kept interrupting, batting down my words with easy confidence. I looked at Maddie sitting next to him on the sofa. Her discomfort was obvious, but she said nothing. *Let it go*, I read in her eyes, so I stopped arguing with him. He did a kind of verbal victory lap, gleefully trashing poor people in general, their laziness and lack of ambition.

"He's attracted to wealth and power," Maddie told me afterwards. "He sees poverty as weakness. Empathy is not his strong suit."

Maddie was much more tolerant than I. She disagreed with Rafi about politics and people, and was frustrated by his brute sense of superiority, but she accepted him as Other. "He worked his butt off to get where he is," she said, "and he has disdain for anyone he considers lazy or inept." She shrugged. "I love him. But he's a completely different creature from me. Sometimes I look at him, and have no idea how I've stayed with him so long."

When they'd first met, Rafi had been drawn to Maddie's aristocratic New England family, while Maddie had wanted nothing more than to get *out*.

"As a kid, I was starved for love," she said. "It wasn't on the menu growing up." Her parents had not been particularly interested in children. What they wanted was an *heir*. Instead, they got three girls, before finally having the son they'd been waiting for—Maddie's younger brother. "I was more privileged than you can imagine," Maddie said. "But I thought my only chance to be loved was to marry a man."

As a teenager, she told me, she fell head-over-heels for Rafi. "He was nothing like anyone I'd ever met. I was completely crazy about him. Obsessed." She smiled, remembering how she could think of nothing else but Rafi; she couldn't focus on her studies, didn't care about her grades. She spent hours day-dreaming about him, writing out her name in cursive letters in her notebook: *Mrs. Madeleine Brinley Rabinovitz .... Mrs. Rafi Rabinovitz ... Mrs. Maddie Rabinovitz ...*

I had a hard time wrapping my head around that. Maybe it was our age difference and upbringing—my parents were hell-bent on getting me through college and graduate school and settled into a professional career before they would even entertain the notion of my getting married. And even then, they made it clear that I must never marry at the expense of my career. They needn't have worried. I, myself, had no interest in becoming anyone's wife, and in any event, no one had any interest in making me theirs. Had I met Maddie when she was a teenager, I would have considered her a bubblehead for chasing after a man.

★ ★ ★

Now, on a hillside in Swannanoa, I learned that her long marriage had been riddled with the bullets of Rafi's chronic infidelity. He'd always been rather casual about commitment, Maddie told me. From the very beginning, when she ran off to Israel at nineteen, he'd made it clear: he would not marry, he would not be tied down. He had to be free of all attachments at all times. "Here's what I plan to do," he would say whenever an idea popped into his head. "You should join me if you want. Or not. Up to you."

He was always hankering for adventure. She, on the other hand, was thoughtful, more cautious. But she admired gutsiness, so she pushed herself to follow him—far beyond the comfort of her affluent upbringing. She loved him, she said, precisely because he was so different from her; life with him would never be easy, but it would be wild and exciting, if she could just manage to hang on.

"I mean, I know he loves me," she said. "But basically, he charts his own course, follows his own compass. He'd never consult me about his plans." If she didn't join him, he was confident he could always find other women to pick up and deposit along the way. He liked to think he didn't need anyone or anything.

It would be years before they finally married—on a lark, she said—in Boston after flying from Jerusalem to spend Christmas with Maddie's family. The marriage proposal was made by neither Rafi nor Maddie, but by Chase, who had been plotting to get her younger sister to tie the knot. On New Year's Eve, 1969, Rafi and Maddie finally agreed. Chase quickly found a justice of the peace in the Yellow Pages. "She woke him up in the middle of the night, drove us to his house through the snow, and half an hour later, we were married."

Maddie shook her head. "And within six months," she said, "Rafi was sleeping with one of my best friends."

How could she put up with it? I wondered. *And what on earth did she see in him in the first place?* I kept quiet and let her continue.

Not only could Rafi not be tied down by anyone, she said, but he also eschewed owning, or even carrying, *things*. He needed to have his hands free, unencumbered by a briefcase or tote bag, in case he had to leap a tall building. He couldn't be held back by practicalities. Those were for his staff—his wife or girlfriend, his secretary, anyone but him. He traveled light, cash in the pocket of his jeans. *Hold this for me, will you?* he'd say, handing Maddie his billfold. Or a sheaf of papers. Or his keys. Whenever they went out, she was the one to carry his stuff. When he went on shoots, his assistant would carry them. "He never takes a suitcase anywhere," she told me. When he traveled (and he traveled all the time) he'd carry a shoulder bag with a change of underwear, his toothbrush and razor, perhaps a spare shirt or two.

"It goes back deep with him," Maddie said. Back to when he was a child—he and his mother were constantly on the move, never staying in one place very long, lest their cover be blown. After the war came further upheavals: DP camps, temporary housing in one place or another, until they landed in Paris. Then to Israel, where once again, his mother didn't stay long before moving back to Paris and Rafi moved in with his best friend's family.

"He's always been like that," she said. "He doesn't want things. They tie him down, they make him feel trapped."

Rafi and I were somewhat alike in this regard, at least when I was in my thirties. We both seemed to feel the need to be ready to escape at any time. Neither of us could quite trust the continuity of our lives in any long-term way. To be able to hop in a car or on a train or bus and start over somewhere else. In those days, I always carried a knapsack with wallet, keys, wool shirt, Swiss Army knife, and a small first aid kit, as if at some point during the day I might find myself on a glacier in the wilderness.

Maddie and Rafi had, in fact, traveled around the world in the early '70s. They'd roughed it for months, slept under the stars or in makeshift huts, hitched rides, took buses, rode on carts drawn by water buffalo, whatever local transportation they could find. Asia, Vietnam, Haiti. It all sounded terribly romantic and adventurous to me.

At some point in the '70s, after a decade together, Maddie started pitching the idea of having children. She'd always wanted kids. Rafi did not, because nothing screamed *Tied down!* quite like having a child. But in keeping with his laissez-faire attitude, he eventually agreed not to stand in her way. He was happy to contribute the starter seed; she was welcome to have kids and raise them if she wanted. He would of course, contribute financially, but caretaking would be her job.

As it turned out, Rafi was swept off his feet by his two daughters; he fell hard for them. He'd never imagined that for all his ambition and accomplishments, what he'd most needed in life were his kids.

But even after the kids were born, his affairs with women did not stop, they did not pause. "Literally a girl in every port," Maddie said. "You'd think he'd be embarrassed by his lack of originality."

She cut her eyes at me, and I could practically taste the bitterness in her voice.

"Why did you put up with it?" I asked.

She shook her head slowly.

The sun was beginning to sag under the weight of winter clouds. "Let's walk," she said. It was already late afternoon as we headed back across the hardened farmland to campus.

I'd never liked Rafi much before, and now he dropped several floors in my mental parking garage for narcissistic men. He had no redeeming values, I thought. Ok, he was a Holocaust survivor, and I would cut him some slack for his traumatic childhood, but he was still a selfish wolf. And it angered me to think that Maddie had put up with it for so long. Looking back now, I'm amazed at how naïve I was. I'd never been in a long-term relationship, and I'd never really considered all the complicated reasons why couples stay together.

★ ★ ★

After the readings that evening Maddie and I returned to the dorm to prepare for the next day's classes and workshops. After an hour or two, she called to me, and I popped my head in her room. She was sitting cross-legged on the twin bed, leaning against the concrete block wall by the window. Her notebooks and papers were spread around her.

"Come in," she said. "Close the door." She capped her pen and pushed the sleeves of her black sweater up to her elbows while I closed the door quietly.

"Here, sit down." She made room for me on the bed, stacking her papers and placing them on the floor.

I sat facing her. "What's up?"

She looked at me with an embarrassed smile. "I don't know how to say this, so I'm just going to say it."

I nodded. I thought maybe she wanted to talk more about Naomi. I would have talked with Maddie about anything she wanted, for as long as she wanted.

"I'm in love with you," she said.

My breath caught in my throat. In an instant, my surprise turned to elation. I hadn't seen this coming, had never even imagined it possible, but now that she'd spoken, it seemed so obvious: light dawning on Marblehead. I was Marblehead.

"I've felt like this for quite a while," Maddie said, her voice quiet but urgent. "I just didn't know what to do with it. I didn't know how to make sense of it." She leaned forward. "What are you feeling?"

I tried to say something, but I couldn't find any words. What was I feeling?

"I'm in love with you, too." As if a wall had been knocked down, there it was: the truth I'd worked so hard to deny. I'd been in love with her for the past year, but it felt like half my life. I'd just never allowed the feelings to rise to consciousness. Why was I always the last person to know what I was feeling?

She leaned forward and our lips touched. Softly, gently, a release from one state of being to another: from functioning, rational people into lovers. I felt myself swept up on wind thermals, as if my lips had become wings. Then all the symphonic side effects: lights popping up in various regions of your brain, the swell of music somewhere in your ribcage, the twinkle-toes of joy running up and down your spine.

We drew back for a moment, then our lips closed in again. I touched her face with my fingertips, she touched mine. A sense of relief, everything releasing exactly as it should, a sense of letting out the sails, letting go of all the guardrails.

She straightened her legs and pulled me down beside her. We fit together as if our bodies had known all along that we belonged together, the effortless perfection of physics. But when she started fumbling with my jeans I stopped her.

"No, wait," I said. "Let's slow down. I don't want to rush this."

She looked amazed; her eyes, green and gold-flecked, filled with wonder.

"I just ... You're married. I can't do that again. I mean ... Let's take our time."

She sighed, and we lay together in each other's arms, happiness spreading over us like bright watercolors. What bliss, to be wrapped up in each other like this, floating far above the earth and its tenacious gravitational hooks. It was as if we'd been straining against invisible chains, and we'd finally broken free. We could just drift in each other's arms.

I don't know how long we remained like that, but at some point before dawn I kissed her and went back to my room. I dropped off to sleep, but kept waking with a smile on my lips, wondering, *Is this a dream? Am I in a dream?*

CHAPTER 6

We returned to Boston, exhausted but exhilarated. The taxi dropped us at her curb and for the first time, we hugged goodbye. "See you soon," she said. "I'll call you."

Returning to work felt like crashing into the hard edge of reality from a great height. My office, as usual, was warding off attacks from legislators and various factions of the private bar; Maddie's kids were starved for her attention; Rafi was heading off on another trip to research his new project. I stacked my notebooks, handouts, and faculty assignments on my desk, hauled two loads of laundry to the coin machines in the basement of my building, and waited for Maddie's call.

We made a date to run around the Brookline Reservoir three days later. It was cold and gray, the snowbanks crusted with dirt. I took the afternoon off from work, rushed home, threw on sweats and an old sweatshirt, and met her at the corner of her street. My stomach did a little backflip when I saw her. She was stretching her hamstrings, one foot raised on the wrought iron fence, her legs impossibly long in black tights.

"So how are you doing?" I asked as we started down Harvard Street at an easy clip.

She groaned. "I'm going nuts. I feel like a teenager. How about you?"

"Same." We laughed.

Traffic picked up as we reached Brookline Village, forcing us to jog in place at slushy intersections before picking our way across the street and heading south to the reservoir.

"So what do you want to do?" I asked.

"I can't go this long without seeing you," she said.

My hands tingled, as if her words had danced directly from my ears to my fingertips. "Well me, neither, but ... I mean, long-term, what do you want?" I'd been up the last three nights, obsessing over how Maddie and I could pull this off. My affair with Carla still haunted me. Falling down that elevator shaft of love had taught me that I was constitutionally incapable of hanging out on the Mezzanine of Amour—casually riding the elevator up to the second floor for breezy sex with a lover, while going about my business on the ground floor. No, I was the sort of gluttonous lover who *had to occupy the whole damn building* with my beloved. Nothing halfway.

I'd told Maddie I needed a long-range plan. I couldn't be with her unless she decided to leave Rafi, so everything now depended on what *she* wanted. I was afraid to pressure her or get my hopes up.

"I want to be with you," Maddie said.

I grinned, happy, but cautious. "What about Rafi?"

She was quiet. Her breath puffed out in soft white clouds. "I'm going to leave him," she said. I've wanted to leave him for a long time. Our marriage is ... I mean, I love him, but our marriage is impossible."

I'd seen enough of Rafi to believe that being married to him would be impossible for anyone. It bothered me that Maddie had put up with him for so long—what did that say about *her*? I didn't dwell on the thought, but in my fairy tale mind, I imagined rescuing her, me in my shiny suit of writing armor (ream of paper as my shield, fountain pen as my sword), saving her from her insensitive, womanizing brute of a husband.

We crossed Route 9 and ran up the short pitch to the reservoir. The mile-long loop stretched out before us, rimmed with frosted maple and cherry trees. A few geese paddled serenely on a narrow strip of glassy water, but most of the reservoir was frozen solid.

"What about the kids?" I asked.

A runner in a Red Sox hat flew past us. "That's just it," she said. "I have to figure out a way to do it. You know, with as little disruption as possible." We were quiet for a moment, our steps falling in sync, our breaths pluming before us. "It's going to take time," she said.

Something about her tone of voice—flat and hard as the back of a hand—made my throat tighten; my rescue fantasy evaporated. *Kids?* What was I thinking? How could I break up a family with *kids?*

"Listen, I'll understand if you don't want to leave him." I threw the sentence out to see how it sounded. It sounded false— an arbitrary toss of words to the wind, a frisbee flung into the distance. The fact is, I couldn't understand why she was still *with* him. But the idea that she might now leave him for me was both thrilling and terrifying. Thrilling because I wanted nothing more than to be with her. Terrifying because in my heart of hearts, I didn't think I was worthy of her—and certainly not worth breaking up her family for. I couldn't take on that responsibility. The guilt would kill me.

If not the guilt, then Rafi. Certainly Rafi would kill me.

Bottom line: I felt like a sham—holding myself out as a bona fide lesbian and ostensible adult, when in fact, I'd reached the age of thirty without ever having been in a real, live, committed relationship. I should come with a warning sign: *Student Operator.*

I didn't say any of this.

"I don't want to break up your marriage or mess up the kids' lives," I said instead, as if reciting from the Book of Noble

Intentions. "So if you leave him, you have to do it for *your* sake, not just to be with me."

She nodded.

I was pleased with myself; I thought I sounded like a rational person. "Because if I'm the only reason you leave him, it'll never work. That would put way too much pressure on us ... on our relationship. You know what I mean?"

What I meant was I was chickenshit.

Hard-packed snow crunched under our feet. She seemed to be figuring something out in her head. I couldn't tell if she was listening.

"So pretend I'm not even in the picture," I said. "Let's assume you and I just stay friends, nothing ever happens between us, ok? Would you stay with Rafi, or would you leave him?"

She stopped running and turned to face me. "I already left him once before," she said. "But I got suckered back in. I know better now. This time I'm leaving for good."

* * *

The last time she'd left for good was five years earlier, in 1984. She told me about it as we walked home from the reservoir. Alarms should have been going off in my head. *She'd managed to leave him, but went back?* Instead, thanks to my staggering naïveté, I felt encouraged, as if she'd done a test run and now, finally, was ready for liftoff.

They'd been living in Boston, Maddie said, since Rafi had accepted a job as a producer at the Boston PBS station a few years earlier. But she was growing more and more unhappy; she missed her life and friends in Israel. The girls were not yet in school; Rafi was never at home—he was off working, traveling, fucking other women. At some point, Maddie told me, she'd "had enough." One day, after threatening to leave for a long time, she finally packed up the girls, bought plane tickets, and moved back to Jerusalem.

It wasn't only Rafi's philandering and ceaseless affairs that had gotten to her, she told me. Looking back, she realized that when she'd first met him in 1964, he was already starting to gravitate away from Israel and toward the States; part of her allure was that she was American. In her novel, Rafi's fictional character says of Boston, *It's so peaceful here, like a permanent holiday. No bombs, no terrorists, no security checks.*

Maddie, on the other hand, had found Rafi beguiling because he seemed dangerously foreign. Perhaps even more than falling for him, she fell in love with Israel—a sunblasted war-torn slice of land as harsh and far as she could get from her patrician Boston girlhood. Their paths had coincided for a while, but by 1984—some twenty years later—it seemed they were headed in opposite directions, each more attracted to the country from which the other came, rather than to the person they'd first fallen in love with.

I don't know the details or exact timing of her leaving him— whether she stormed out with the girls one day and he pretended not to care, or whether she left him a note while he was out of town. In any event, Maddie and the kids settled down in Jerusalem, and reunited with their friends. And a new development: a man whom Maddie had known for years was deeply in love with her. Like Rafi, Omer was well-educated and highly respected in his field. But unlike Rafi, he was considerate, faithful, and put Maddie at the center of his life, a new experience for her. They moved in together.

Seven months later, Rafi flew to Israel and showed up at her door. He begged her to come back.

"I was done with him," she told me as we waited for the light at Cypress. It was mid-afternoon by now, and the low-hanging sun hit us full in the face. We had to shade our eyes with our hands in order to see the traffic light. "I was not about to go back after all I'd gone through." But she agreed to hear him out, and he managed to break her heart. "He went down on his knees, Maddie said. "He was crying. I'd never seen him on his knees in my life, and I'd certainly never seen him shed a tear."

I, too, had a hard time imagining Rafi doing this. His pain—or his pride—must have been excruciating for him to break down like that. Then again, it also struck me as manipulative, but I stayed quiet.

"He begged me. He said that the girls and I were his only family in the whole world. He had lost everyone in the Holocaust, we were all he had."

I recognized the power of this plea. Throughout my life, my mother had always reeled me back into the fold of our family when I had set out on my own. My life, I knew, was nothing compared to the losses that she and my father had suffered during the war, and for this reason, I felt compelled to honor their wishes more than the need to find out who I was and live my own life.

Maddie paused, remembering the moment. "He said he'd been an idiot, having affairs left and right. He hadn't realized till now how important I was to him; how important *family* was to him. He said his life had no meaning without me and the girls. And he promised he would never be unfaithful again, if only I would come back to him."

She shook her head. "Poor bugger," she muttered. "I really had moved on. I'd made a new home for us. Omer was a good man. I loved him, and he loved me—no, he *really* loved me—and I knew that he would never do what Rafi had done to me. And I was happy living in Israel, I loved Jerusalem, Naomi was there, and so were our friends, and the girls loved it there. I thought we would never leave."

We were approaching her street now, and she offered to walk me back to my place. The girls wouldn't be home for another hour, and Rafi was still at work.

"I think it was the part about being Rafi's family—his only family in the world—that got to me," she said. "My heart went out to him. Because I've always felt that about him—he was like a wounded animal, and I've always felt the need to take care of him, to give him a sense of family that he'd never had. His childhood was nothing but hiding and hunger, constant fear. He'd lost everyone except his mother, and their relationship was stormy all his life. So I felt responsible, in a way. I felt I owed it to him, that the girls and I really were his only family, and that he had finally woken up and *gotten* it. He finally seemed to understand that he had to treat us like his family. He couldn't just do whatever he wanted, and expect us to be there for him when he decided to show up."

She was quiet for a moment. "So he persuaded me."

We reached my door, and I invited her in from the cold. We sat on the tiny plaid pull-out sofa in my living room.

"I told Omer that night," Maddie continued. And of course, he was heartbroken, and I felt like shit. But I really believed that Rafi had changed. I'd never seen him like that. I felt I had to give him another chance."

So she and the girls packed up their belongings and returned to Boston with Rafi. They moved back into their Brookline home, determined to make a fresh start. Rafi continued to work long hours at the PBS station, but he now seemed to be more considerate and attentive at home. Maddie could see that he was making an effort.

A few months after returning to Boston, Maddie learned that Rafi was sleeping with yet another woman.

"I was batshit," she said. "Just furious." She drew her lips in a tight line. "It's like he *waited* till I'd landed a new job, till the kids were settled in school and made new friends. He knew I couldn't pick up and go back at that point."

In a fit of pique, Maddie decided to have a revenge affair. She started dating a man she soon regretted enlisting for the role; she took no pleasure in stooping to Rafi's level. But she did succeed in making Rafi so angry, he agreed to go to couples counseling with her. Of course, the minute she broke up with the man, Rafi stopped showing up at couples counseling, and resumed his affair with his girlfriend.

★ ★ ★

Maddie, I should have said, *what are you still doing with him now, in 1989?*

I'm raising our kids, she would have said. *I'm writing a novel. I had my chance. The girls are in grade school; they're happy with their friends and activities. I can't yank them back and forth to Israel like that. I have to learn to live with it.*

But we said nothing. We sat in silence on that plaid little sofa, and then we were kissing. It seemed to happen *to* us, this kiss, this embrace, this fondling. I don't remember either of us initiating it. At some point we just found ourselves in the middle of each other, our hands everywhere, our tongues everywhere. It was no one's fault, no one's doing; we were simply moving with the current of the river.

Eventually I managed to catch myself—perhaps I'd thrown my hand out and hit something solid—the armrest of the sofa, maybe—which set off an alarm in my head and brought me back to reason, back to my dumpy little living room. I lurched up. "We can't do this; we have to stop."

Maddie, too, opened her eyes, came up for air, and whispered, "Shhh," before pulling me back down with her. I realized I was no match for such elemental forces. How did we manage to resist the power of our attraction, the urgency of it? Why didn't we just fuck our brains out?

Perhaps my fear of losing control, of literally drowning in love, is what kept me trying to surface. At last I managed to disrupt the flow of things until we managed slowly, slowly to pull apart, till our lips were just barely grazing each other's cheeks, and then just our fingertips grazed each other's lips, and then we finally somehow separated enough to pull our pants up and our shirts down, and we managed to stand, then stumbled a bit and leaned against each other again at the door, and then started again, it was so easy to lose myself like this, to fall back into the stream of things. Intention is no match for passion.

But fear is. Fear brought my words back to me, and made me repeat them like a mantra. *We have to be patient. We have to wait. You have to leave him first. We have to wait.*

It seemed forever, it seemed a day or two later, but it was only minutes—she slipped out my door and went back to her home.

* * *

This scene repeated itself over the following few weeks, no matter how disciplined we tried to be. On the drive home from our writer's group, she'd pull over at the curb and our hands and tongues would be all over each other. Or she'd stop by my apartment in the early evening, and we'd find ourselves on the little plaid couch. I soon lost my resolve and caved. "Maybe it doesn't matter after all," I said one afternoon, wrapped in her arms, slipping my hands under her shirt and unfastening her bra. "Maybe waiting is stupid." Moments later she stopped me. "No." She pulled back. "No, this isn't smart." It occurred to me then that she was as scared as I was. Maybe we were both too chicken to go through with it.

What were we so afraid of? Why such Herculean self-restraint?

I was still recovering from self-immolation after my affair with Carla the year before. Maddie's circumstances—older, married, kids—were freakishly similar, only worse. (At least Carla's husband had been fine with her having a girlfriend; Rafi, I knew, would go ballistic.) Even I, with my remarkable gift for denial, could not set foot in the same fact pattern twice. I needed to wait until all husbands were cleared from my path.

If I'd learned anything from Carla, I told Maddie, as we walked around the reservoir the next day, it was that my heart was a snowflake, I was no good at sharing, and I was going to get stomped. At thirty, I had the emotional maturity of a teenager, while Rafi, at forty-seven, was more like Charlton Heston in Ben-Hur. I would not emerge from this chariot race in one piece.

"I'm over here in my little toga and sandals," I said. "And he's barreling down in his leather-strapped chest, reins in hand, grit on his brow."

She laughed. "He's actually quite a softie."

"Right," I said, rolling my eyes. A group of runners flashed by, a blur of bodies.

"No, really. He just comes on strong."

"The point is," I said, "I can't be in the ring with him. I can't share you with him."

We fell silent for a moment. "Let's jog," she said. But a minute later she slowed back down to a walk. "You know, what

I'm most worried about is the kids. I can't bear the thought of blowing up their lives."

I nodded. The certainty of destruction—a horrible, colossal domestic conflagration—was a sure thing. I felt I should warn her. "Custody rights suck for queers," I said.

Any lawyer Rafi hired would certainly raise Maddie's "lesbian lifestyle" as a reason to deny or drastically limit her custody of the girls. Rafi, himself, felt that lesbians should be kept away from children; he told Maddie that he didn't want me anywhere near his kids unless he was present. Scores of eminent child psychiatrists and psychologists supported his views at the time, and courts, dependent upon precedent, have always been conservative by nature. I'd done a research paper in law school in 1980 on the custody rights of homosexuals: *The odds on getting custody are greater than ninety percent against a woman who has had a lesbian relationship.*

"That was nearly ten years ago," I said. "But still, even if you win custody, it would wreak havoc on Rafi and the kids."

Maddie winced. We continued walking in silence. I pictured us sitting in the dark-paneled Norfolk County courtroom across from Rafi and his lawyer. All exits guarded by snickering court officers.

"I don't know if I can do that to either Rafi or the kids," Maddie said. "They adore each other. I can't imagine reducing their relationship to some court-ordered schedule."

We started jogging again, beginning our second loop around the reservoir. My stomach churned at the thought of lawyers and judges and child psychologists; the division of assets, shuttling the girls back and forth between us, the rancor, the rage. Maddie and I had better be sure of what we were getting into, before we ventured any further. We'd need time to

make a plan, stock up on supplies, start sewing our flame-re-
sistant suits.

★ ★ ★

Over the next few days and weeks as we wrestled with our
decision, we talked about all of this. How would we deal with
the complications of living as a lesbian couple raising two young
daughters in Boston in 1989?

"I don't know," she said when I raised the issue on our run a
few days later. She never asked me about the lesbian community,
and I sensed her reluctance to become a citizen of Queerlandia,
just because she'd fallen in love with me.

"I'm not sure I'm like that," she said, when I mentioned the
Pride parade.

"Like what?"

She shrugged. "I don't know. I think I'm more private. I
don't need to make a political statement of it."

I nodded, realizing how little exposure she had to the gay
community. Few straight people did in those days. I didn't want
to scare her, so I didn't mention some of my own experiences of
homophobia. Obviously it was easier to be queer in Boston than
in Alabama or Idaho. But walking down the streets of Boston,
I'd been shoved and called a fucking dyke. (Maybe homophobes
had better gaydar than I gave them credit for.) Once, walking to
the T at night, a car full of guys drove by—they seemed to patrol
the area around gay bars—and yelled *Get fucked, dyke! A cock'll
cure you!* They spat at me and threw beer bottles before peeling
off. Glass shattered on the sidewalk. My stomach twisted, as if
a hand had reached in and yanked me, churning fear and rage.

It could even happen at work. A lawyer whom I supervised
called me a lesbian pervert and threatened to report me to his

state legislator who obviously shared his views. "I'll have your job!" he snarled into the telephone. I didn't think he'd get very far, but the venom in his voice curled inside my brain and took root.

And it wasn't just the open hostility that got to me. Many of my straight friends said they had no problem with my being queer, but they objected to gays walking hand-in-hand in public. They agreed that consenting adults should be free to do whatever they wanted in the privacy of their bedroom, but gays and lesbians should not be teachers or work with kids.

And of course, in Boston, as elsewhere, the children of lesbians were often ostracized and ridiculed at school—not only by their classmates, but by teachers and staff. Were Maddie and I prepared to put the girls through that?

I didn't say any of this, afraid to tip the scales against me.

It occurs to me now that Maddie was overwhelmed by everything—by the fact that she had fallen in love with a woman, the fact that she'd never imagined leaving Rafi for a lesbian, the fact that she was comfortable in her straight social milieu and that she felt no particular affinity for, or even curiosity about, the gay community. She had too many obstacles to cross before she could get there.

At the time, I was just beginning to see how straight and strict and white and sheltered her 1950's childhood had been. She still carried so much baggage from that time—a full-luggage set of her Boston Brahmin upbringing, including a sense of propriety, an obligation to be pleasant, and a deference to men—all of which, even now, she was still unpacking and trying to shed. On top of that, she'd spent seventeen years in Israel, an even more macho, misogynistic, and homophobic land than America.

Do something that scares you every day. Maybe breaking up the kids' lives was too scary for me, and far too scary for

Maddie. She was about to become an emigrant to a foreign land in her own hometown. Did she know what she was getting herself into?

Our friendship, I thought, was too important to risk. We had the rest of our lives to be together—it just made sense to take our time, to be sure of what we wanted, and to consider how it would play out, before doing something that couldn't be undone.

* * *

Abstinence makes the heart grow hotter, and reduces the mind to rubble. A few weeks later, she and Rafi were going away for a long weekend, and it became apparent that I was now going to lose my mind. I forced myself to take deep breaths and eat leafy green vegetables between gallons of ice cream and chocolate. The next day, in addition to my morning swim, I went for a run in the afternoon and then added a weightlifting session at the gym at night. I wrote in my journal obsessively. Minutes oozed by like sludge. On Sunday evening I wandered through the local grocery store when I caught a glimpse of her at the entrance, her long black coat flapping open, Spanish leather boots, and my heart—I swear my heart leapt across Aisle 7 toward her. That moment when our eyes met—the half-smile on her lips a meteorological moment, the tidal pull of the ocean, the whole seashore of feelings sloshing through me. She'd been away for, what ... two days? She wasn't due back till tomorrow, but here she was, just entering the store as I was leaving, and we wanted to—but couldn't—do anything about it, there was the public to think about, appearances and propriety and secrecy and holding our breaths. She was still married to him. She wasn't sick yet. It was winter. The tumor hadn't yet knocked on the door of her frontal lobe.

CHAPTER 7

Looking back now, thirty-five years later, I feel I've come upon the scene of a car crash. Tapping on the keyboard as if operating the Jaws of Life to extricate my mangled younger self from a vehicle in a state of continual implosion.

It didn't help that back then I couldn't bring myself to confide in anyone about my affair with Maddie. I was ashamed of my apparent inability to trawl for love anywhere but in Straight Mommy waters. What was wrong with me?

I certainly wasn't about to tell my lesbian friends that I was in love with yet another married woman. They had been impatient with me two years ago when I'd fallen for Carla, only to be crushed by her limited availability as wife and straight mother. *What did you expect?* they said. They'd picked me up, dusted me off, and introduced me to their queer friends; they dragged me along on lesbian outings, insisted that I stick to the gay community, steer clear of heteros and married women. It was Lesbian 101—*Stay the fuck away from straight women*. Period. If you disregarded this basic principle, then you were an idiot, and you deserved the misery you were about to receive.

If I hadn't fully appreciated this before, I certainly knew it in my bones after Carla. The problem, of course, was that the world was practically crawling with straight women. It's not like I went out looking for them, but you couldn't *avoid* them; they were everywhere. Meanwhile, the tiny lesbian community cycled through the same group of friends and lovers over and over, which creeped me out. Besides, I seemed to be more attracted to feminine women, which further limited the shopping aisles in the lesbian community.

I was too ashamed to tell my gay friends that here I was again, doing the same damn thing. And since I'd never talked with my straight friends about my life as a queer, no additional effort was needed for me to keep Maddie a secret from them. They knew her as my "friend," a word that took on enormous weight in those days.

Back then, I wasn't even out to my parents, whom I revered. They were no more curious to know about my love life than I was to tell them. Sex and romance were never discussed in our family; romance was considered an unwanted distraction from the primary goals of life, which were:

1. Family loyalty;
2. Academic excellence;
3. A wildly successful career in law or medicine.

My mother viewed even my ordinary garden-variety friends as threats to my primal loyalty to our family. In my parents' view, *no one* but immediate family could be trusted. This principle had enabled them to survive the war and the Siberian Gulag. But apparently it precluded me from ever starting a family of my own, since anyone I dated was, per se, a dangerous outsider: *verboten*. The orthodoxy of my family trumped even the orthodoxy of the lesbian community.

So that left my therapist, Lisa, with sole responsibility for steering me through the mess I was in. I'd been in therapy with her for five years now, and I was a hard case. Lisa was blonde and stylish, with clear blue eyes and a striking resemblance to the young Glenn Close in *Fatal Attraction*, minus the perm and the knife. (Lisa's hair was wavy; her voice soft.) On a scale of zero to hot, she was sizzling. As I recall, we were not getting along too well at the time, Lisa and I. I'd been in love with her, too, for my first couple of years of therapy, and although it was probably a huge relief for her to finally get me over *that* hurdle, I wondered how she, a straight woman, would be able to help me with my affair with Maddie. Over the course of my lesbian adolescence with Carla two years earlier, I'd increasingly come to feel that Lisa just didn't quite *get it.* Yes, of course, she was perfectly accepting of me as gay, but for all her earnest, over-educated, liberal good intentions, she still didn't quite grasp the reality of queerdom.

I had trouble explaining the insularity of the lesbian community, the desperate need for places like lesbian bars and women's concerts in which to let loose. It was hard to describe the strain of conforming in a straight world, the constant editing of oneself in accordance with your immediate location. Among straight friends, you were careful not to mention anything about your queer life, or say anything revealing a queer perspective. With gay friends, the relief of peeling off the straitjacket of self-restraint meant you could point out girls who looked hot, gossip about who was dating whom, discuss politicians, judges, professors, celebrities, who were queer but closeted. But on the T, you had to be careful not to touch your women friends or sit too close to them, opting instead to stand to avoid suspicion.

In the office among straight staff, you would "sanitize" your story of going to a party with friends, careful to omit the fact that it was a queer event or at a gay bar. You would never refer to your partner as a "partner," but as a *friend.* If you lived with her, you called her a *roommate.*

In the courtroom, of course, you had to act not just straight, but also *feminine.* You wore skirts, stockings, pumps. (This was years before the discovery of the pantsuit by Hillary Clinton.) Court was the province of straight white men in those days— from the judges, clerk magistrates and prosecutors, to the court officers, cops and probation officers. To do right by your client, you had to talk to all these players as a straight feminine woman. Smart white women who flirted strategically were extremely successful in court, just as they were everywhere else in life. (It helped to be drop-dead gorgeous, of course, but this was beyond my control.) My lesbian trial supervisor encouraged me to get the best deal for my clients by schmoozing with the cops. "Of course, you'll need to shower afterwards," she said dryly.

In public, you were careful not to call attention to yourself; always just a bit on guard, looking out for the random guy who would shove or yell at you, the random car that would pull up and throw a bottle.

And most of these adjustments were subtle and smooth and unconscious, but the cumulative effect of all that carefulness resulted in an inordinate need to blow off steam from time to time, to run naked through acres of fields with a thousand other lesbians at the New England Women's Music Festival, for example, or to let down your guard in a gay bar or at a gay resort.

Perhaps Lisa, in her zeal to champion the rights of gays, naïvely believed that lesbians were righteous liberals who believed in equal rights for *all* people at all times. So when, flushed with excitement, I told her about my first women's music festival, she bristled at my delight in excluding men from these settings. Wasn't that unfair to men? Shouldn't lesbians, of all people, want to include *everyone* at their festivals?

Never mind, I wanted to say. Defending the right of lesbians to be human was not helpful.

But in Lisa's defense, in those days, I moved through the world with a built-in queer alarm system, never stopping to examine, much less put into words, how I felt or how I operated within these constraints. I didn't have to explain anything to gay people—they just *knew*, it was a quality of life we shared, and it made for an instant connection, even if we had nothing else in common. I was afraid I would not be able to make myself understood—perhaps I didn't understand myself—the elaborate gymnastics involved in protecting myself as a lesbian from the world in the 1980's. Through my silence, I left Lisa and my straight friends in the dark.

Of course, when I think of myself back then, I realize that as a white, unremarkable-looking woman, I always had the option of passing. Even today, I see everyone making adjustments—gay, straight, BDSM, surgeon, or gunnery sergeant. We all have to camouflage certain aspects of ourselves in order to live in the world. Depending on one's job, most people are not free to act and dress at work as they do at home. If you want to have a face tattoo, you may have to give up your dream of being a trial lawyer in Omaha. I was a public defender in Boston, which meant I could be out at work, even if I felt the need to be circumspect about it. I suffered far less from these constraints than gays in traditional law firms or other businesses. I didn't have to sacrifice much of my freedom of expression for a paycheck. Or for acceptance. Or to avoid ostracism, hatred, violence.

I was lucky, fairly clueless, not particularly woke.

The line between denial and passing can be fuzzy. For years I was in denial of my queer identity precisely because I was capable of passing. I'd had boyfriends, after all. So convincing was my own act, my carefully constructed straight mask, I wasn't even aware that I was in hiding. All I knew was that something was very wrong with me.

★ ★ ★

Weeks slipped by as Maddie and I wondered what to do with our blossom of love, first offering it sunlight, then scuttling it back into the closet. Finally one Friday in February, as we walked around the reservoir—we didn't even pretend to run anymore—Maddie and I both seemed to have come to our senses at the same time. We agreed to put our love on hold—at least physically—until she had finally left Rafi. We walked home, feeling a bit sad to have succumbed to good sense, but proud of our decision.

"We have plenty of time," I said when I left her at her doorstep and continued to my apartment. "There's no rush."

We agreed to meet two days later at eleven for a Sunday run—a real run, now that we had both agreed to refrain from touching. "Finally we can get back in shape," she laughed.

Sunday morning I put on my sweats, worked on a story, and waited for her call. The sky was flat and gray, a typical February morning. It hadn't snowed in over a week and the streets and sidewalks were clear. A few minutes after eleven the phone rang. But it wasn't Maddie; it was her sister Chase.

"Something scary has happened," she said. "Maddie had a seizure last night. She has brain cancer. She's in the ICU at Mt. Auburn, and she asked to see you. You have to say you're her sister. They won't let anyone in but family."

I remember my heart, a hammer. I remember my hands shaking. I had to concentrate on breathing. I didn't really feel anything—just a sudden, drastic narrowing of possibilities. Everything became very simple and straightforward: We weren't going for a run. I changed out of my sweats into jeans. I looked at a map to find the fastest route to the hospital. I threw my knapsack over my shoulder, locked the door, and walked the mile down Harvard Street to my Ford Escort, which I parked in a colleague's driveway for a monthly fee.

There was no traffic. I took the Eliot Bridge across the frozen river—a bridge I knew by heart from rowing in the Head of the Charles regatta in college. It's the last bridge before the final sprint to the finish line. Driving to the hospital felt a little like that—a surreal sense of heightened awareness, with the finish line receding around the last curve, certain but unseen.

I felt calm—perhaps numb is a better word—as I entered the hospital, asked for Maddie, and told the staff I was her sister. It was a little creepy, how kind everyone was. I walked down the corridor feeling strangely disembodied, my head floating above my body, barely registering my footfalls on the linoleum. Bright lights, beige walls, the muffled sounds of hospital staff moving past me. I felt nothing, as if my feelings had been whisked away to some padded cell offshore, inaccessible.

I reached the door to her room just as Rafi was leaving. We paused a moment, standing a few feet from each other, speechless. We nodded in greeting, our eyes lingering just long enough to exchange a look of profound sorrow—and it was then that I felt something like a kick in the gut. His gaze broke through my calm, and I sensed, for that split second, that our world had crashed, that he and I were now somehow together, both adrift. Then he was gone.

* * *

Maddie's long figure lay in antiseptic white sheets. Surrounded by blinking lights and tubes, she could have been an art installation. She opened her eyes and smiled at me with such warmth, my heart soared. All the medical equipment, the hospital johnny with its little blue doo-hickeys, fell away, and I felt the silly uncomplicated joy of love. I sat on the chair next to her and took her hand in mine. We both grinned at each other stupidly for a moment.

"Hey," I finally said.

"Hey."

"You know, if you didn't want to go for a run, you could have just said so. You didn't have to go to such extremes to get out of it."

She smiled. "*Now* you tell me."

"How are you feeling?"

"Fine." Her face was so beautiful, I could almost forget everything else. "Tired," she added. "Just really tired."

"Can I get you anything?"

She shook her head.

"Do you remember what happened?" Chase had told me that she and Maddie had been together at a party at a friend's house in Cambridge the night before. Maddie had been standing in the living room, holding a glass of juice and talking with a few people when she twisted slightly to the side, her hand went out, the glass fell, and she collapsed to the floor.

"Not really," she said. "I remember before the party, getting dressed, putting in my contact lenses ... and I remember going there, but then I can't really remember what happened."

We sat quietly, holding hands.

"This is such bad timing," she said, smiling.

Brain cancer had no manners.

The ICU nurse came in, checked the leads, went out.

"Hools," she said, suddenly serious. "I can't do this without you." She called me Hools. Also Hoolie, Hula, Lulie.

My heart brimmed. I smiled. "I'm right here. I'm not going anywhere."

"But you know ... We agreed ..."

"Shhh," I said. "No rules."

"No rules?"

I shook my head. "The rules are out the window."

"Because I can't leave him now."

"Of course not. Don't even think about it. None of that matters now, ok?"

She nodded.

"We're in a new land," I said. "We can do whatever we want."

She tightened her grip on my hand.

"I'm right here," I said. "I'm all yours."

* * *

She was transferred the next day to the Brigham for a battery of tests and scans. They gave her a big room, bright and sunny, on the 12th floor, with a sweeping view of the western suburbs. I arrived mid-morning carrying a passel of goofy knick-knacks and wind-up toys I'd bought at Brookline Booksmith—pink kangaroos with boxing gloves that did back flips when you wound them up; small plastic action figures which we used to stage melodramas on her tray table, etc. Rafi and the girls arrived soon after, and all of us—Rafi included—played with the toys, happy to be distracted from the prospect of brain surgery. Maddie's laughter was infectious, and it was nice to see Rafi smile—in all the time I'd known him, I'd rarely seen him playful like this. His broad face lit up, and I caught a glimpse of the rascal that Maddie loved.

We kept everything light, joked around and teased each other, and although it was a bit of a production, we managed, in the face of the auto-da-fé of brain cancer, to convert horror into humor.

* * *

Anaplastic astrocytoma. It figures that she would grow star-shaped cells in her brain, with a name that rolls off the tongue. It's a sure-fire killer, but if you bombard it with the entire arsenal of modern medicine, you can postpone the inevitable for two-three years—coincidentally, just long enough to get an MFA.

This was our window, although she and I never talked about her prognosis. There is nothing quite like a death sentence to give you permission to live. Maddie and I seized our newfound freedom and ran with it. Death put all our prior fears to shame— my fear of losing my heart, my fear of facing Rafi in court, our fear of hurting the kids—none of that mattered by comparison. Brain cancer gave us permission to be lovers in whatever time she had left.

New land, no rules.

CHAPTER 8

They gave her one week to get her affairs in order; surgery was scheduled for early March. I took the week off from work so I could be with her all the time. As a state employee, I had a ton of vacation days at my disposal. My boss, Anita, allowed me to take the time on short notice, and ascended to sainthood in my mind.

Maddie decided her first order of business was to get a haircut for herself and for the girls. Rachel's long hair was thick and wild; Eva's was buttery blonde. Since the surgeon would be shaving the front half of Maddie's head, she wanted a short haircut to get used to the look. She made an appointment with her hairdresser around the corner, and the four of us trooped over.

He cut the girls' hair first, and within forty minutes, they looked glamorous, their long hair luxuriously styled. He took more time with Maddie. She had a beautifully shaped head, and the simple cut suited her. I riffled my fingers through it. "I love it," I said. "You look adorable."

★ ★ ★

Maddie later wrote an essay for our writing program, noting,

When we were all done, my girls, skipping ahead of me down the sidewalk, looked so neat and well groomed—like someone else's children. And I had a cut I knew why I'd avoided

all these years. My sister comforted me with compliments about the attractive shape of my head. I felt so good about the girls' haircuts, maybe the way an animal mother feels after a good grooming of cubs. The girls seemed happy, too.

★ ★ ★

The week before surgery flew by. We hung out at her place, making meals and lists of things to do, running errands, and goofing off with the kids when they came home from school. In the evenings we watched comedies, the sillier the better: *Beetlejuice, Airplane, Ghostbusters, Ferris Bueller.* Rafi, as usual, was away during the day. Work, he later told me, was a lifesaver for him. He poured himself into a new project, a documentary series on Columbus, requiring an enormous amount of research, writing, and international travel.

Chase, in the meantime, contacted their childhood nanny, Jo—an Irish woman who had worked for their parents as a teenager. Now nearly sixty, Jo lived nearby; her own children were already grown and out of the house. She agreed to come back and work as cook and caretaker for the girls, once Maddie went in for surgery. Jo adored Maddie and the kids, and Maddie often told me that she had felt closer to Jo than to her own mother. Jo, she said, was warm and caring; Constance, not so much. As a child, Maddie often went downstairs to the maids' quarters to seek comfort from Jo.

Maids' quarters.

Maddie later wrote that she thought of her brain tumor as a sort of cosmic reckoning for her privileged upbringing:

"Maybe why I got it in the first place: I had too many breaks before. My life until the age of 41 had only the merest

difficulties, an imbalance of ease, an affluent fluidity, where trusting parents drew up trust funds every time they sat down. I wouldn't call it blessed, but there was little to complain about."

* * *

With friends and family dropping in and out all day, Maddie and I hovered close to each other. Neither of us could bring ourselves to talk about what would happen next; we counted down the days, not knowing whether she would survive the operation, and if she did, what would be left of her. *What if I woke up and didn't know myself or my children?* she later wrote.

"I've had a good life," I heard her tell a friend over the phone. "I've traveled around the world; I feel very lucky." She paused, and I wondered, *How can she face death at the age of forty-one with such self-assurance?*

"Oh, I know," she was saying now. "I know all about cancer." Her mother and father had both died of cancer. Rafi's mother had died of cancer. She made it sound as if she were some kind of expert, uniquely qualified to die of cancer.

Me, I was a novitiate. Yes, I'd lost friends to cancer—even brain cancer—but they'd died off-stage, in other cities, enabling me to grieve from a safe distance.

Besides, I had not been in love with them.

* * *

The afternoon before surgery, Rafi brought her to the hospital. Peter Black, the neurosurgeon, came by and talked about the operation. After Rafi left, I came in, sat on her bed, held hands. Night had fallen. The lights of the city filled her window.

Dr. Black, she said, had explained that he would try to remove as much of the tumor as possible. But because of its star-shaped cells, and its tendency to shoot tentacles into surrounding brain tissue, he would need her help during the operation. She would have to remain awake during surgery, so he could communicate with her and ensure that she was able to respond when he ventured into parts of her brain affecting speech, movement, vision, and so on.

Do you prefer to lose sight, or speech? he asked. *Do you prefer to lose muscle control, or speech? The ability to walk or to speak?*

He spoke gently, with enormous kindness, she told me. But she'd never had to consider questions like this before, and it was unnerving to do so on the eve of surgery. Dr. Black told her that he had his own ideas about what choices he would make, but he wanted to honor her preferences. She decided that most important was her ability to comprehend language and to speak; next was movement, and finally, eyesight. He smiled. "That's what I would pick, too," he said, and for a moment, she felt she had won the brain surgeon dating game. She was then given endless pages of informed consent documents to sign, stating she knew she could die from the operation; she could wind up blind, paralyzed, speechless, etc.

I managed to keep quiet while she told me this, but I felt a silent scream forming in my throat. It seemed barbaric to have to make these choices. And to lie awake with your skull broken open so you could tell the doctor what you're feeling when he touches part of your brain with a metal probe. The whole thing was diabolical, something out of Frankenstein.

"I'm scared," she said.

"I know." I didn't recognize my voice—I sounded freakishly calm. "But here's the deal. If you get through this operation, we can do anything we want. Ok? All you have to do is get through the surgery."

She nodded.

"You're going to do great. You're going to sail through." I wished I felt even a tiny bit as confident as I sounded. I was amazed at what a bullshitter I was.

"Hools ..." she said. "You'll be there when I come out, right?"

"Of course. We just have to get through tomorrow. Then we're home free."

"No rules?" she said. "We don't have to behave ourselves?"

I laughed. "God, no! Only bad behavior from now on."

★ ★ ★

I didn't sleep. I got up early, put in my usual laps at the Allston Boys and Girls Club, then met Chase for a walk around the Fens. We were both out of our minds with anxiety. Walking helped. We distracted ourselves by telling stories to each other. As we walked for miles along the Emerald Necklace, Chase told me about her childhood and teenage years, about her relationship with Maddie, about Chase's stint as a visual artist before becoming a scientist; about her falling in love with Andy and their lives as academics—in Cambridge, Paris, Kyoto. Chase was a masterful storyteller, and her voice was calm and soothing, and I clung to her every word. In this way we managed to hold our anxiety at bay, never once mentioning brain cancer or surgery.

In the afternoon we stopped to make a call: still no word. A terrible pressure was building, as if my body could no longer contain my nerves and I would break apart. I stayed very close to Chase, afraid to be alone. Finally we learned Maddie had come out of surgery and all had gone well. Dr. Black said he got the bulk of the tumor, and we could visit her in the recovery room that evening.

The room was dimly lit, spooky. She lay in a nest of tubes, her head wrapped in an enormous turban of gauze; her cheeks puffy, eyes closed. We spoke softly to her, cooing. She didn't respond, she wasn't conscious.

She was alive.

★ ★ ★

During surgery, the neuro team had unceremoniously pulled the flap of skin down over her face while excavating her brain. Swooping in with their ropes and clamps and scalpels like mountaineers, extreme skiers; shredding the gnar. Then they packed up their gear and went home. The trail they'd cut through the dome of her head remained, and the next morning they returned to admire their work, to assess how closely they'd shaved their course, carved their turns through the gates of the wily astrocytoma, leaving strips of healthy tissue behind, rags flapping in the wind.

★ ★ ★

The following day she was moved up to a room on the twelfth floor with a bright wall of windows. She was groggy but awake, with a massive headache. She could see and talk, move her arms and legs. None of the horrors we had feared had happened. Rafi, Chase, and I took turns at her bedside—I took the early morning shift, came back at noon, and again late at night. The nurses on the neurosurgery floor were impossibly kind, and pretty much ignored the hospital's visiting hours altogether. I told them I was Maddie's sister, and they let me come and go at any hour of the day or night.

* * *

Maddie later wrote in an essay:

Waking up from general anesthesia after the operation was one of the worst feelings in the world. I was nauseous, disoriented, and terribly anxious that a headache might be lying in wait, ready to ambush me if I turned my head too quickly or tried to sit up. A big bandage was wrapped around my head. All I wanted was to hug my middle sister [Chase], who with her ferocious optimism always refused to hear my complaints. I wanted her telling me that I would feel better in time, but I also wanted to tell her that all I wished to do at that moment was die. That feeling quickly passed. She would have been right: there is nothing like the human body recuperating, and general anesthesia wearing off. If a religious person had told me it was God's work, I'd have been converted.

* * *

Maddie was on steroids to reduce the swelling in her brain, and by evening, she was wired, unable to sleep. She asked me to stay, and we ended up talking all night: about our childhoods, our families, her life in Israel, the serendipity of our initial meeting. (As it turned out, we'd both attended the same writing conference the fall before our summer workshop at Harvard.) And we talked about how we would find time to be together after she was out of the hospital and I was back at work. We never spoke of her prognosis—from my own research, I knew she didn't have more than two or three years to live. I assumed she, too, had been told this, but I decided never to talk about it unless she raised the issue. She never did.

The hospital had gone quiet, her room dark—it was around three in the morning, when she motioned for me to lean in closer. I thought she wanted to whisper something in my ear, but instead she kissed me, and pulled me toward her. She took my hand, guided it under the sheet. She looked at me searchingly, then closed her eyes. I studied her face; she smiled when I slipped my hand under her johnny and slowly, carefully, quietly, made love to her for the first time.

After so many weeks of Good Girl self-restraint, this was not how I'd envisioned our first time. My heart twisted sideways. I began to appreciate how gut-wrenching our affair was going to be. Eventually I withdrew my hand, and just as I did, Dr. Black appeared in the room. I leapt off the bed as if shot by a cannon. He greeted us with a smile, sat down in the space I had just vacated. "It's warm," he said, his voice kind, looking up at me. I was mortified.

"How are you feeling?" he asked Maddie.

What the fuck was he doing here at this hour? If he'd come a minute earlier, he would have caught us *in flagrante*. Sitting on Maddie's bed now, he spoke softly, asking whether she'd been able to sleep, reassuring her that she'd done beautifully and she'd be home soon. *He couldn't have seen anything,* I told myself. *The room was dark; he would only have seen my back.* Maddie and I later agreed that he was the kindest, most gentle soul we'd ever met; it seemed impossible that he was also a surgeon. As we discovered over the following days, Dr. Black basically never stopped working; he came by to see Maddie a few times a day, sometimes in the morning, sometimes in the evening, sometimes in the dead of night

* * *

When they removed the bandages, a zipper of flesh stretched across the top of her head, almost ear to ear, not quite symmetrical. A few small divots here and there that bothered me, as if the surgeons had pressed a little too hard in places while stitching her up.

I slowly ran my fingertips alongside the seam, so lightly as to barely register as touch. The nerves had been frazzled, and when I traced the line with my fingers, it seemed to soothe them. Her eyes closed. Her brow unfurrowed. She smiled when I leaned in close and blew air softly along the line of the scar. I spent hours at her bedside like this, lightly touching her head.

* * *

The tumor had been the size of a small grapefruit, Dr. Black told us. *How do you fit a grapefruit in a frontal lobe?* I wondered. His teammate described it as the size of a man's fist, an image I found even more disturbing. It had been growing for many months, if not years, squooshing the healthy tissue, until finally the pressure built up to the point where it caused an electric storm in her brain.

Usually, Dr. Black said, before a seizure finally announced the tumor, one experienced auras; Maddie now realized that she'd had her first aura a week or two earlier. She'd been driving me home one night from our Cambridge writing group and we took the BU bridge. A traffic island divides two lanes at the major intersection on the Boston side of the river—a triangle of concrete with a streetlamp and traffic light. As we came across the river, Maddie seemed to be heading straight for the street-lamp on my side. "Maddie!" I finally cried. My left hand shot out for the steering wheel. She quickly corrected, and we lurched back into our lane. "Sorry," she said. I was amazed at how calm she was; my heart was racing, my arms spaghetti-like from the rush of adrenaline. I said nothing, not wanting to make her feel bad, but I was miffed that she hadn't been more concerned.

Now she told her doctors about it. "I didn't know what was happening at the time," she said. "I was in some sort of trance. It was the strangest thing—I was conscious, but felt suspended, like I was floating."

Surprisingly, neither Dr. Black nor any of her neuro team suggested she stop driving after they sent her home after surgery. She was on tons of meds: anti-seizures, anti-inflammatories, anti-biotics, all intended to ensure her safety. But less than two weeks later, while driving a few blocks from her house, she had another seizure ... causing a head-on collision with an oncoming car.

I got the call at work and flew out of the office. It was a beautiful day—sunny, breezy, warm, and as I sprinted to the hospital from the T station, I wondered how everyone could be going about their business as if nothing had happened. Even the weather was unconcerned—the sun smiled blithely on the mag-nolias along the Muddy River.

She's ok, Chase had assured me over the phone. *No one was hurt.*

Chase's idea of what constituted "hurt" was different from mine. You didn't wind up in the hospital if you weren't hurt.

I found her lying on a bed behind a curtain in the ER—dazed but—Chase was right—not hurt.

I caught my breath, leaned over and kissed her. "Are you ok?" Under my suit jacket, I was bathed in sweat. I mopped my brow with a tissue.

She nodded. "I'm fine. They just want to keep me here a few hours 'for observation.'" She made air quotes with her fingers, and I could see she wasn't attached to any tubes. "I'm just tired. They gave me more sedatives."

We held hands. Her fingers were so long and thin. A plastic hospital band circled her wrist.

"So what happened?"

"Oh Hoolie, I feel terrible. Rachel was in the car with me. And a friend of hers." Maddie winced to think of it. "They're fine, they're back home. But Rachel saw the whole thing happen, and she's pretty upset."

I ran my fingers along her brow. "It's ok," I said.

She shook her head. "It's not ok. Nothing is ok."

★ ★ ★

The accident: Maddie had been driving rather slowly in heavy traffic on the main drag, I later learned. *All of a sudden*, Rachel said, *Mummy slumped behind the wheel*. The Jeep drifted over into oncoming traffic. The other driver hit the brakes, but couldn't avoid impact. Maddie, unconscious, was the only one taken by ambulance to the hospital.

Just a few weeks ago, none of this would have been imaginable, but now, in the spring of 1989, every time the phone rang we all braced for catastrophe, and wondered which hospital we'd have to go to.

Maddie was horrified that she'd had kids in the car. The doctors increased her anti-seizure medication, and now warned her not to drive.

A time would come about a year later, when Maddie rebelled. She hadn't gotten behind the wheel since that accident, but one afternoon in 1990, Maddie called me at work. "I'm driving out to see my therapist." Defiant. Unless a friend gave her a

ride, she always took a taxi. (This was decades before smart-
phones or rideshares.)

"Oh Maddie," I said. "Please don't."

"I can't live like this."

"I know, it sucks. But I can be there in half an hour. Let me
drive you."

"Nope. Gotta go."

"Then call a cab. Please. There are other people out there,
other kids in other cars."

"I'll be fine," she said. "I can do this."

I begged, I argued, I pleaded.

"I'll go crazy," she insisted. "I just have to do this."

I finally got pissed off. "Then why did you call me? Just so
I'd worry?"

"I wanted to let you know," she said.

"Well, I don't want to know. If I can't drive you, and you
won't take a cab, then don't call me. Do whatever you want, but
don't tell me, so I won't have to worry."

We hung up. Maybe it was good, I thought, that we could
get angry at each other. We'd been under so much strain for so
long. It wasn't healthy, a relationship in which you didn't fight.
Of course there was nothing healthy about our relationship.
"Unhealthy" was built right into our operating system. Our
affair began with a death sentence.

She drove herself to therapy. She drove back. Nothing happened. As far as I know, she never drove again, but she said she'd
needed to prove to herself she could do it. She was a grownup.

★ ★ ★

Ironically, during her first semester of the writing program—a year before her accident—Maddie had written a story

inspired by her elderly father who had gotten into a fender bender not far from Maddie's own accident. At the time she'd written the story, her father was no longer alive, and Maddie had no idea that an astrocytoma was already spreading its stars through her brain. In her story, the father drives his beloved Alfa Romeo slowly home from his country club in the rain. He sees a blur of red in the rearview mirror, and fears he's hit something. Afraid to stop, he continues, certain he'll be arrested, but nothing happens. At home he examines the scratch on the car, and realizes he has to give up driving. He decides to give the Alfa to one of his sons. In real life, Maddie told me, when her father had to stop driving after a minor accident, it marked the beginning of the end for him—the loss of his autonomy, his independence, and his sense of self.

★ ★ ★

Two weeks before Maddie's car accident, back in March, 1989, while she was still in the hospital recovering from her craniotomy, Rafi had come to visit her and begged her to go with him to Cannes for the film festival. I was sitting on one side of the bed, he on the other. I felt uncomfortable around him and wondered how to make a graceful exit. "It's not until May," he said hopefully. "You have plenty of time to recover." She took a deep sigh. "I don't think so."

He smiled. "Think about it," he urged. "It will be so much fun. You don't have to go to all the events. You can rest in the hotel room whenever you want."

She closed her eyes. He glanced at me, and I hoped my face didn't betray my feelings. *Are you nuts?* I thought. Maddie hated the Cannes Film Festival on her best day. Over the years, she had sometimes succumbed to his pleas, because the festival was his favorite thing in the world. But she hated all the hoopla, the beautiful people, the fancy parties, the wretched excess. If ever she had a valid excuse to skip Cannes, this was it.

"We'll see," she said, and fell back asleep.

★ ★ ★

Later, in one of her essays, Maddie wrote:

He kept asking if I was ready to travel yet. I finally communicated clearly that even if I was, I didn't want to. Could he go then? Was it really ok? Yes, of course. I could be generous when the alternative was going with him. But as his departure date drew near he became sadder and more anxious. One day, quite rare tears flooded his eyes and he said, "I know that I can get away from this horrible thing that has happened to you by traveling. I know that under the pressures of work, I will forget—but I guess I know, too, that you can never forget it, or escape it." I said that was true.

★ ★ ★

At some point before he left for Cannes in May, Maddie finally told Rafi that she was in love with me. Did she say we were *lovers*? That we were having an *affair*? "I didn't go into detail," she said. How did he take it? She shook her head and wouldn't say more.

I admit, I was a little afraid of what he might do. He did not strike me as someone who let things slide. On the other hand, I was a mere girl, an annoyance, hardly a threat. I didn't even feel particularly significant to *myself*.

CHAPTER 9

He went to Cannes and I spent every moment I could at their apartment. I was both shocked and relieved by his absence. How could he be so indifferent as to leave her and the kids at a time like this? Maddie shrugged it off. "His work is good for him," she said. "And he loves Cannes." She smiled. "More time for us."

I loved goofing off with the kids, practicing worm rolls on the floor with them, discussing the pros and cons of invisible personal space travel, etc. We took turns "styling" their hair into ridiculous shapes. We created wild fashions from household items, wearing pillows as hats and stringing spoons and forks around our waists. Maddie was an easy-going mother, self-assured, a natural.

At the time, I had no idea what went into being a parent, since my identity was so firmly entrenched in being a daughter. I'd never been the least bit interested in having kids myself, and I'd never been blindsided by the biological urge that gripped so many women my age. It would have been impossible to grow up in my family and think that having children was a good idea. "If I'd known what it would be like," my mother had once told me, "I would never have had children." I'd been surprised by her honesty but not by her sentiment. After all, our family life had been a nightmare. My father used to say that enduring six years in forced labor camps in Siberia was better than spending a day in our family. Instead of feeling offended by this remark, I'd felt validated.

I was pretty sure I'd be a terrible parent; I'd wreck any child's life. I was too self-centered, too impatient, too needy. But now, hanging out with Maddie and her girls, I found myself—for the first time in my life—*wanting* to have kids with her—and not just any kids; I wanted *these* kids. My heart was expanding with love like the Goodyear blimp. Maddie told me she often indulged in a fantasy of a lesbian paradise for us—a small yellow cottage near the ocean with side-by-side Hers & Hers writing studios, Rachel and Eva with us.

* * *

Before the 1980's, coming out as a lesbian almost always included coming to grips with the fact that you would not have children. Even if you already had biological children from a prior marriage, you risked losing custody, since homosexuality—like heroin addiction or prostitution—was considered evidence of your unfitness to parent.

Things were beginning to change by the time I met Maddie. "Lesbian Partners Find The Means to Be Parents" ran a headline in *The New York Times* in January, 1989. The article quoted professors of psychiatry and psychology, however, warning that children raised by homosexuals would have serious difficulties with intimacy later in life, and would face other "perilous" consequences. The following month, a "correction" was made to the article, saying these professional opinions had not been sufficiently researched.

In any event, Rafi was dead certain that I, as a lesbian, should be nowhere near *his* kids unless he was present. When he returned from Cannes in May, Maddie told me, he was furious that I'd spent so much time with the girls. Apparently Rachel and Eva kept talking about all the fun we'd had in his absence. It drove him nuts. "He admitted he couldn't prevent me from being friends with you," Maddie said. "But he didn't want you around the kids." She smirked. "As a lesbian, you will damage them in unimaginable ways."

"What did you say?" I asked.

She shrugged.

I didn't press her, but my outrage at Rafi ballooned. *If he cared that much*, I thought, *why does he leave her and the kids alone half the year? It's ok for him to be an international playboy, but he wants to dictate who sees his kids in his absence?*

★ ★ ★

And I'll admit it: there were times, especially back in the beginning, when I wished the tumor had shot its stars into *his* frontal lobe and not hers. After all, we'd just launched, Maddie and I—we had so much promise, we were just blasting out of the starting gate. Brain cancer was practically a laughable plot device, the schlocky twist no self-respecting screenwriter would throw into a story.

It would have been much simpler and more convenient for Rafi to get the brain cancer. He was built for the part—he could belt out that theme song—the harsh, arrogant producer, humbled by his own mortality, comes to appreciate the devotion and love of his wife and kids. His colleagues, whom he's bulldozed throughout his long successful career, now honor him with a Lifetime Achievement Award. He's wheeled onto the stage to a standing O, the clapping and cheering rising to the rafters. He grins, his eyes filling with tears that spill down his scruff onto his collar. The collar his wife lovingly buttoned for him hours earlier, his coordination lost to the muddle in his head...

No. That particular fantasy was a crass inside production, made by me, for me, a bitter audience of one. I would never breathe a word of it to Maddie. It was in poor taste. Shame on me and my selfish evil heart.

But still.

* * *

While Rafi was away, Maddie and I started going to a brain tumor support group that met at the hospital on Thursday evenings. After a while we quit because it was just too depressing to watch one new friend after another die so quickly. They'd be cracking jokes one week, and a few weeks later they'd be having trouble walking. The next week they'd be in a wheelchair, and soon they were gone altogether. New brain cancer patients came to take their places, with the same scared look we recognized from our own faces a few months ago. I kept trying to prepare myself for losing Maddie. But of course you can't; you always have to lose someone in real time. She started a six-week course of radiation later that spring of 1989. We made a schedule, and friends took turns driving her to and from the hospital, down the elevator to the cavernous sub-basement of the Brigham. Whole-brain radiation: five young techs in scrubs clustered around and positioned her under the beam.

In a short essay submitted as part of her graduate thesis, Maddie wrote:

I lie, hands crossed on my chest, on the glass table. Technicians finger my thinning hair and tape my chin for mask-like stillness. "Perfect, perfect," they say to each other.

"Beautiful." For the first day or two, I took it all to heart, felt good, felt it was a compliment. I didn't care if it was programmed to make the patient feel good. But no, they were talking about aligning the dots tattooed on my head with the position of the beams. I do want "Perfect," too. There are all kinds of complicated systems in there that I would rather not have messed with.

The techs leave the room, she closes her eyes. She can hear the machine rev, then sees a cobalt blue flash under her closed eyelids each time:

Like some brilliant medusa on its side, its trailing tentacles cup my eyes, she wrote in the essay. *Warmth, tingling, no pain. Just a question about the wisdom of all this.*

They are back: smiling, chatting, teasing each other, continuing some conversation they started in the control room. Back to the Perfects, Beautifuls, and zapping from other angles. It's all the same, really, not so hard to take. "Stay still, don't move," are not commands that frighten me. Only, sometimes my heart beats so hard it flips over.

By the end of the six weeks, she was dog-tired, slept all the time, could barely hold a book to read. Our writing program had adjusted her deadlines, enabling her to continue to work on her stories and essays on a revised schedule. It never even occurred to her to take time off from the program. Unlike writers who choose to make a career of writing, Maddie and I (and most of the Warren Wilson students) had loved to write, but had chosen other careers for various reasons—financial, family, or practical considerations. Now in our thirties and forties we returned to writing with a passion, almost with a vengeance. We were born-again writers, on fire to make up for lost time.

Maddie was determined to complete her MFA in whatever time she had left.

* * *

Returning to Warren Wilson in July, 1989 for our fourth residency after such a tumultuous six months felt strange. Everyone was thoughtful and kind, careful and inobtrusive. I didn't leave Maddie's side, except to bring her food from the cafeteria when she was too tired to go herself. Toward the end of the residency, she and I planned an overnight getaway to the tiny town of Hot Springs, Tennessee, an hour away. We left right after morning workshops and arrived at a scruffy inn in a torrential downpour. An old mountain man seemed to be the only soul in town. He checked us in while scratching the gray forest of his beard, then shuffled off and seemed to disappear into the woodwork.

We headed out for a soupy two-mile hike on the Appalachian Trail to a rock outcropping called Lover's Leap. The guidebook had promised panoramic views of the French Broad River and Pisgah National Forest, but the rain had other ideas. Between downpours, we gazed out at rags of mist, but most of the time we stared down at our soggy boots. Still, it felt good to be out in the mountains together, away from everyone and everything. We could almost forget about her cancer, her husband, my job, the rest of the world.

We returned to the inn, completely drenched. The wooden floors creaked as we took the stairs, peeled off our wet clothes and climbed into the giant claw-footed tub together. We took turns slowly washing each other. Time stretched. Each moment felt generous, like stepping into a grand museum and giving ourselves over to our senses, every inch of skin gently touched, soothed. It wasn't so much erotic as calming, an intimacy that breathed, explored, unfolded and opened. The rest of the world drifted away and even her brain cancer seemed to evaporate into the cloud of steam rising from our tub. The seam across her skull was nothing more than a work of art, a tactile sensation. In those hours we were together, I luxuriated in the sense of having enough, of being enough, of wanting for nothing.

The next morning we were back on campus in time for the nine o'clock classes, and said nothing to our classmates of our illicit getaway. Our absence must have been felt—we were a very tight group after all—but to our relief, no one said anything.

★ ★ ★

A few weeks later, Maddie's first faculty supervisor, Allan Gurganus, invited her to his book party in New York, celebrating the publication of his much-anticipated novel—a sweeping history of the American South. Allan was not only a sweetheart of a man, but also a literary Wunderkind whose book would become a blockbuster, winning prestigious literary awards and selling over four million copies, riding high on the NYT bestseller list for eight months, and being made into an Emmy-winning miniseries. His book party was to be hosted by one of the most renowned and beloved literati in New York. It was a Very Big Deal.

"We're going," Maddie said, handing me the beautifully embossed invitation on cream-colored paper. "We'll have to find you something to wear."

I feigned insult. "I have plenty of things to wear!"

She stared at my black sneakers. "Shoes," she said. "Do you have any *shoes?*"

I did not have shoes. The Spanish boots she had me buy last winter would not do for summer.

We made a deal: I would take care of our travel plans, and she would take me shopping for shoes. She picked out a pair of designer two-tone olive suede/brown leather wingtips, which she instructed me to wear with my light linen slacks and a knit top. I reserved us seats on the shuttle, in-and-out, same day. We counted down the days.

Allan's party was a chance to get away together, a small pearl of time when we could be out as a couple—shucking the burden of pretense we shouldered at home. We flew to New York in the morning and spent the day together, then cabbed it to the party on the Upper East Side, before flying home that night.

We seemed to have teleported to a parallel universe in which Maddie and I could hold hands in public; we could be ourselves. Of course, I was out and Maddie wasn't, but no one knew her in New York—we were anonymous, we could do whatever we wanted, without fear of word getting back to anyone she knew in Boston.

The freedom was even more intoxicating than the spectacular view over the East River from the host's grand apartment. I was so enthralled by having Maddie to myself, I registered very little of the party, though I remember the host's boyish flop of silver hair over his forehead, his big smile and erect posture when he welcomed us inside; Allan, beaming, gave Maddie and me a warm hug, before gliding off to greet others. I gaped at the rooms of antique furniture and Oriental rugs, walls lined with books and paintings by famous artists.

We worked our way to the far end of the apartment and grabbed seats on a settee along the wall. I brought Maddie a small plate of food and a glass of seltzer. We were content to sit together holding hands as the room swirled with people talking animatedly, sipping wine, laughing. A number of young students of Allan's—twenty-year-old kids who looked eager and awkward and barely hatched—talked excitedly among themselves on the sidelines near us. A wave of sadness washed over me, and I felt terribly old, a worn-out wannabe. These kids were on the verge of their lives, just starting out, brimming with possibilities, and I felt as if Maddie and I were at the end of ours. I was maybe ten years older than these kids, but I felt ancient, wizened, jaded. I couldn't imagine my life beyond my time with Maddie. I assumed that when she died, my life would be over. What was the point of anything beyond that? I didn't let myself think ahead.

After an hour or so, Maddie was exhausted. We slipped outside into the warm August night and hailed a cab to the airport. She dozed in my arms. I felt enervated but responsible: paid the driver, checked us in, got us through security, to the gate, onto the plane, into our seats. Maddie slipped into sleep, her head on my shoulder, as we lifted off. The lights of the city twinkled until the clouds swallowed them. How much more time would we have?

★ ★ ★

In mid-August we took our most daring trip—a romantic weekend in East Hardwick, Vermont: The Northeast Kingdom. It was the only time we ran off without even the pretext of a literary event, and without telling Rafi, who was working abroad. I picked the place out of the Gay Guide New England, an indispensable little underground booklet that listed places where you wouldn't get hassled or thrown out when you showed up queer. The B&B was a working goat-cheese-making farm in the middle of nowhere, owned by a lesbian couple who had quit their Manhattan jobs and bought an old farm in the country.

The logistics had been a bit complicated. Rafi was in Europe and the girls were spending the weekend away—maybe off with friends, or maybe something more organized, I can't remember.

Maddie gave her sister Chase the number of the place at which we were staying, in case of an emergency.

By now Chase knew that Maddie and I were more than just "friends;" Maddie had confided in her last spring, not long after her diagnosis. Chase and I had never spoken a word about it, but soon after Maddie confided in her, Chase invited me for dinner at her house, a beautiful turreted Victorian in Cambridge. Before sitting down to eat, she pulled me aside in the pantry. "Listen, Maddie's not gay!" she said, as if this were the most obvious thing in the world. I held my tongue, knowing that Chase was extremely smart, but utterly clueless on this subject. (In fact, she'd tried to set me up with a male friend of hers earlier that year, believing I wasn't gay, either.)

"Well, I think that's up to her," I said carefully, not wanting to upset Chase.

"But, look, she's just not gay!" Chase insisted. "I mean, whatever she's feeling, or whatever she *thinks* she's feeling, it's obviously the tumor. It's not *her*!"

I nodded. The frontal lobe is the anatomical police headquarters of self-restraint—a kind of giant pause button on your impulses. The tumor's location in Maddie's frontal lobe meant that her inhibitions were likely loosened, making it easier for her to feel whatever she was feeling, however "improper" those feelings might have seemed to her before.

"So you think it's the *tumor* that's in love with me?" I smiled. "And not Maddie?

"Well, of course it's the tumor," Chase said. "Maddie isn't gay."

Chase's discomfort with our relationship was understandable. After all, she was losing her younger sister to brain cancer—that was bad enough. But imagining her sister in an adulterous lesbian affair at the same time was just gratuitous melodrama. Chase told Maddie she didn't want to have any part of a coverup for our trip. But finally, Maddie told me, Chase agreed to take the number of our B&B in case of emergency. Luckily, she didn't have to use it.

Maddie and I were bursting with excitement at the prospect of being together in a place where lesbians abounded. We would go for walks, we would frolic with the goats. We would get the fuck away from all the lying and hiding; we would be alone together for the whole weekend.

We arrived at the big white farmhouse in the pouring rain. (Why was it always raining when we tried to run away together? Clearly the gods disapproved.) I found one of the owners in the kitchen, where she was making cheese in large pots. Maddie and I waited for her in the living room—worn pine floors, braided rugs in a mish-mash of faded colors. Old ratty sink-into-me chairs with stitched quilts slung over their backs like burdens, a giant hutch with fresh chopped wood. And one entire wall of floor-to-ceiling bookcases, overflowing with everything from Chaucer and Shakespeare to Betty Friedan and Doris Lessing. It pulled us to it like a multi-colored magnet and we got excited to see all our friends there—Joan Didion, Elizabeth Bishop, Gwendolyn Brooks.

Let's never leave, Maddie said.

I leaned into her and kissed her at the corner of her jaw-bone and ear. I felt her tense. *It's ok,* I whispered. *We're in Lesbo Land.* She kissed me back, tentatively, then pulled back and smiled like a little kid.

The owner led us down a hall to our room at the back of the house. We were the only guests; we had the place to ourselves. As it turned out, it rained the rest of the weekend, and we didn't even care. We pretty much spent the whole time in bed. I made a run to the general store a few miles away and brought back wine, bread, cheese. Maddie had little energy to go out for a hike anyway. We were happy simply to be together. In a few days, I would turn thirty-two; this was my birthday gift.

* * *

In the fall of 1989, my parents came to visit me for a weekend. I was eager to show them off to Maddie (I'd always considered my parents to be the most interesting thing about me) and Maddie was equally keen to meet them. I also wanted my boss, Anita, to meet Maddie and my parents. These were my four favorite people in the world, and I wanted to gather them together like a bouquet of flowers.

Maddie and Rafi decided to throw an informal party Saturday evening for their friends, my parents, Anita, and me. Rafi was eager to meet survivors from his hometown, so the morning before the party, my parents and I went over to spend a little time with them. We sat at their sunny kitchen table and Maddie offered us tea. My parents and Rafi spoke Polish and laughed, poking fun at the time-honored hunting parties at the estates of Polish aristocrats. A tradition completely removed from anything my parents or Rafi had ever experienced, but a safe touchstone for them. *We are from this area, we know this culture, we speak this language that no one else in the world would know.*

My mother talked animatedly. People always gravitated to her, and I could see Maddie and Rafi respond. The discussion wound from Poland to Paris (Maddie and Rafi had lived there while his mother was alive) to art and literature and music. My father, as usual, sat quietly, taking everything in. Every so often he would add a comment or respond to a question, but he let my mother carry the ball, which was how they generally worked their way down the field of social engagements.

When we returned that evening for the party, I luxuriated in the twin beams of my mother's and Maddie's attention, as they stood together, each holding a glass of wine as a prop (neither was much of a drinker) and talked about me with affection. I am ashamed to recall how greedily I lapped this up. It was a kind of wet dream, to have my mother and Maddie gazing at me and joking about how I could have reached the age of thirty-two without having the first clue as to how to apply a coat of lipstick.

Somewhere else in the apartment, my boss, Anita, was hitting it off with Rafi, whom she later declared to be the sexiest man alive.

After a couple of hours, my parents and I walked the two blocks back to my apartment. I was bursting with pride of my family, my boss, my friends. My parents had enjoyed themselves, and my mother was smitten with Maddie. "She's such a *lady!*" my mother effused. "So elegant, so sophisticated." She shook her head with admiration. "And so intelligent and well-spoken!" I liked seeing Maddie through my mother's eyes. Yes, I thought, this was my mother, impressed by a Class Act. My father was more a man of the proletariat. He liked my friends well enough, but he wasn't swooning as my mother was. That was fine with me; it was my mother I'd wanted to impress all along.

Maddie had been equally impressed with my parents. "You're so lucky," she said later. "Both of your parents are still alive! And they're so sweet. I loved having people their age— *parents*—in our house. I never see older people anymore."

My parents were in their seventies, and somehow it hadn't yet occurred to me that their lives were finite. Maddie would run out of life long before they did.

"Enjoy them while you have them, Hoolie."

I nodded. She was right, but for most of my life, I'd only been able to "enjoy" my parents by hiding who I was from them. It had been so much easier when I was younger, when I didn't even know who I was or what I wanted. Until my twenties, I'd simply shape-shifted to fit their needs, pretending to be someone I wasn't—their Perfect Daughter. But by the time I was a third-year law student, my façade finally broke down—quite literally, I had a breakdown—and my parents and I were shocked and angered to discover that I couldn't pull off the performance they needed of me. Now, in my early thirties, I'd managed to redeem myself somewhat by getting a job as a lawyer (albeit as a small-time public servant, representing *criminals*—my parents' views were not that different from Rafi's in this regard) and by protecting them from my transgressive tendencies as a writer and lesbian.

"So what did Rafi think?" I asked.

Maddie shrugged. "He liked them a lot. He thought maybe your mother was Jewish, but he really couldn't tell."

It seemed silly, our conjecture that my parents might be Jewish. I was not focused on my own family at the time; I was focused on Maddie and her family.

★ ★ ★

I wonder, sometimes, what Maddie would have thought when I finally learned the truth about my own family's Jewish identity eight months after her death. She had predicted as much when we'd first talked outside the Harvard library that summer of 1987. Her parents were already dead by the time she was writing about them. Would she have approved of my writing a family memoir while my parents were still alive? I don't think so. Maddie was an accommodating person; she deferred to men, and—particularly after her own parents died—to elders.

Unlike me, Maddie had rebelled when you're supposed to—as a teenager—and had run off to Israel without telling her parents. I could no sooner have done that than sprouted wings and flown to the moon. Even now, in my thirties, I was torn by my loyalty to my parents and my first inklings of independence.

If Maddie had been forced to take sides between my parents and me over the memoir I wrote in 1999, revealing their Jewish identity, I fear she might have chosen my parents. In fact, I'd always chosen my parents over me, too, for most of my life, which had been my biggest obstacle to mental health. In a way, losing Maddie would ultimately give me the strength to choose my own truth over my parents' lies.

It also occurs to me now that I never told Maddie about the dark side of my family, about growing up in a mad house, in which my parents' wartime trauma leaked into the fabric of my childhood. I never told Maddie about the ubiquitous threats and attempts of suicide, psychiatric interventions and hospitalizations. Maddie knew, of course, that I was in therapy, that I had struggled with depression and an eating disorder for years, but in the late 1980's, it wasn't just Maddie I was trying to hide my family dysfunction from—I was trying to hide it from myself.

★ ★ ★

Later that fall of 1989, Maddie set out on a full-bore Helen-improvement scheme. Unbeknownst to me, she hired her young housecleaner to blitz through my dingy apartment one day while I was at work. I was thrilled to come home and find Maddie sitting on the plaid couch, a bowl of fresh oranges gleaming on the coffee table. But I didn't even notice that my apartment had been cleaned. Maddie was disappointed to discover that there was only so much you could do with a worn-out hovel with rusted pipes, leaking ceilings, and half a century of city grime embedded in its cracks.

"You have to buy a place of your own," she said. "We have to get you out of here." Apparently she had talked with my mother at the party. My mother had agreed.

"Get your parents onboard, and call a realtor," Maddie said. "When you find something, let me know, and I'll look at it with you."

It would take me several more months before I could imagine becoming a homeowner. My parents encouraged me to look for something "more presentable," than my current digs, and offered to help with the down payment. Eventually I found a condo I could afford in a triple-decker in Jamaica Plain. I arranged for the realtor to show it to me and Maddie. "It's nice," Maddie agreed. "But you can't buy it, Hools. It's too far away. I need to be able to walk to you."

I had, in fact, started my search in Brookline, but there was nothing I could even remotely afford anywhere near us.

"I'll keep looking," I said, but I gave up after a while. There was nothing I could afford in our neighborhood, and neither Maddie nor I could face the prospect of me moving farther away.

A time would come later when Maddie was no longer able to walk to my place; she would push me to look farther, look wider. To begin the unthinkable work of not just moving, but moving on.

★ ★ ★

For now Maddie decided to focus on smaller improvements. "Let's get you a bra or two at Lady Grace," she said one Saturday afternoon. We were hanging out at her place; the girls were out with friends and Rafi, as usual, was at work.

Just the name of this store made my stomach turn. *Really?* I said. *Lady Grace?*

"Shush. It's a great place. It's been there forever, since, like, 1940. My mother used to take me and my sisters there."

I'd walked past the store in Coolidge Corner countless times. Its giant storefront windows displayed old-fashioned mannequins wearing full-length frilly negligees that looked like they were from a Howard Hawks movie set. "I'm not setting foot in that store."

Maddie laughed. "You should do something that scares you every day."

"I'm not scared. I'm ... too immature to appreciate its offerings."

The store employed middle-aged women who were expert bra-fitters, Maddie said. "They're really good."

"You're shitting me."

Maddie looked at me sternly. "How old are you?"

I snorted. "No way is some lady going to fit me for a bra," I said. "I think I can figure out whether a bra fits all by myself."

Maddie rolled her eyes. "You don't even know what a bra is."

I lifted my shirt. I was wearing my favorite sports bra, a purple Champion that was starting to fray a bit, I wore it so much.

"That's not a bra," she said. "That's an ace bandage with seams."

"It's comfortable! It works!"

She lifted her shirt. "*This* is a bra." Black lace, silky texture, straight-up sexy.

I saw her point. "Ok," I said. "That is definitely working for you."

She dropped her shirt. "So we are going to get you a bra. A *real* bra. At Lady Grace."

"Nope," I shook my head. "I'm not that kind of girl."

How much of a girl was I really? The previous spring, I'd let her take me shopping for clothes, but a fancy bra was never going to happen to me.

It occurs to me now, some thirty years later, that if I'd been born a generation or two later, I would have identified as gender-queer. But because of the times, because of my parents, because of the remarkable strength and durability of my iron-clad denial, I simply accepted my lot as female, however disappointed I felt in my body's betrayal of my true boy's nature. In any event, something of that undeniable boy remained; no one—not even Maddie—was going to put me in a girlie bra.

Maddie, of course, only wanted to help me—she saw me as a remedial case, someone who knew nothing about basic appearances. But in fact, I'd always been preoccupied—obsessed, really—with how I looked. It's just that my concern was limited to the shape and weight of my body. As long as I was fit and strong and under 140 pounds, I couldn't be bothered. Makeup struck me as grotesque. It never occurred to me that women put on makeup in order to appear naturally, effortlessly beautiful, with perfect skin.

You could *do* something about that? My skin was the opposite of perfect. Ditto my body, but I knew how to exercise and how to fast, how to punish myself for overeating, how to starve myself into the right size. Beyond these efforts (which were both time- and soul-sucking) I figured I just had to play the cards I was dealt. I had been dealt a female body with crappy skin that broke out every time I got my period. I didn't believe there was any product in the world to improve it.

It came in a tube with a French name, and it was very, very expensive. Maddie bought it for me, and told me to put it on my arms. Seriously? I thought she was smarter than that. Did she really succumb to those stupid ads? It was snake oil, it was throwing money down the Needless Markup sinkhole. It was Lancôme, come to think of it. I felt I was holding a tube of liquid gold. It smelled very sophisticated. It felt good when you rubbed it in. Did it make a difference? I used so little of it, with such reverence and awe, it had no effect, as far as I could tell, except to begin to break down my fortress of resistance to beauty products. The lotion itself didn't soften me, but the fact that Maddie used it, believed in it, and actually bought it for me, softened my attitude toward the world in general.

But I still would not let her buy me a bra. I did not like bras, my goal was to suppress my boobs, not call attention to them.

"What do you have against breasts?" she asked one night when I was at her apartment. Rafi was overseas, the kids were asleep. We were lounging on the brightly embroidered Bedouin floor cushions in the living room.

"Nothing! I love them! Boobs are super nice on other women. But for me …" I shrugged. "They're always getting in the way."

"Like this?" she said, cupping my breast with her hand. She tilted her head and smiled. "Oh, I'm sorry," she said. "Your breast is in the way. I was trying to reach into your soul."

I stifled a laugh, afraid to wake the kids. We waited to see if any sounds came from their rooms. "No, ok," I said. "Sometimes that is the most direct way to the soul. I will grant you that."

"So is this twice as fast? She cupped my other breast with her hand and leaned in to kiss me. The pillows shifted under us. We were just around the corner from the long hallway to the girls' rooms.

"Yes," I murmured. "We've established a correlation." And then we stopped talking and found better uses for our mouths.

★ ★ ★

I always worried that one of the girls might wake up and come down the hallway to find us doing something that would be very hard to explain to them. "We aren't doing anything wrong," Maddie said. "Don't worry."

"Um, it could be interpreted as wrong."

"I get to hold you," she said. "That is not wrong."

"Ok, but kissing could be a problem."

"Right. No kissing. She paused. "Rules, rules, rules. Hoolie, the kids love you. It's ok."

"And I love them," I said. "All the more reason not to freak them out. Or recruit them for the local chapter of the Lesbian Cabal."

She scoffed. "Since when did you get scruples?"

"I'm a very honorable person," I said. "I'm a lawyer."

She gave me a playful shove.

I reached for her. Her arm was so long and thin, so delicious to touch. A smile danced at the corner of her lips. I leaned in to kiss those lips, then thought better of it. The sleeping kids, my honorable scruples.

★ ★ ★

A year or so later, after she was already quite sick, Maddie went to Lady Grace alone and bought me a luscious silk pajama set in sunshine yellow. She presented it to me in a big ribboned box. My jaw dropped.

"Think of me when you wear them," she said. "Just pretend they're me."

Touching them made me cry.

I couldn't bring myself to wear them; they were too precious, too symbolic of her love. (Baggy t-shirts remained my nighttime staple.) Instead, for decades, I would keep these pajamas safe in a drawer where I could worship them without doing them any harm.

CHAPTER 10

January, 1990

We flew back to Swannanoa in January for our fifth residency, two years after we'd started the writing program, almost one year after her diagnosis. She wore a broad-brimmed black bolero hat and made a striking appearance. In class she took it off. From the back you couldn't tell—her dark hair was cut short. But she had become unselfconscious—almost defiant—about the bald half-moon of the front of her head and ear-to-ear scar across the top. *Here I am*, she seemed to say. *Deal with it.*

Our friends and teachers didn't blink an eye. A few would pull me aside now and then to ask how she was and what they could do to help, but in general, our community of poets and writers were people who moved toward pain, rather than away. Maddie was well loved.

We were both about to start our thesis semester—the six-month period during which you picked a literary topic and wrote an in-depth critical analysis. Maddie wanted to focus on Flaubert's *Madame Bovary*. An interesting choice, considering the protagonist is an unhappy wife and mother who has a passionate affair that ultimately ends in disaster and suicide. It was Flaubert's ability to plumb the depths of his heroine's psychology that most intrigued Maddie, and she wanted to bring the same psychological depth to the characters in her own writing. I suspect she was also looking for herself in Emma, a disillusioned housewife trapped in a marriage that failed to live up to her romantic expectations.

I decided to analyze Louise Erdrich's use of lyricism in her novel *The Beet Queen*, a book that swept me off my feet with the sheer power of its language. Early in the book, one of the main characters, a young bisexual boy, leaves the orphanage and enters the seminary, where he purposefully walks the grounds, pretending to read religious texts, while in fact attracting the attention of hoboes in the bushes. Reveling in his sexual allure in his "slim black cassock," he exploits the aesthetics and symbolism of religious devotion in order to hook up with men.

While I imagine Maddie identified with a frustrated French housewife, I seemed to see myself in a gay orphaned boy in lust. We would spend our semester studying how Flaubert and Erdrich had cast their spells on us.

Two months later, in March, 1990, about a year after her craniotomy, Maddie's doctors called her in to discuss their plan. They knew the tumor would be coming back, and they wanted to *beat it to the punch*. Dr. Black was there, but he took a back seat, explaining with a smile that he was Old School. He introduced Maddie to her new lead neurosurgeon, a tall handsome young man named Eben Alexander with a boyish shock of dark hair. Two other doctors on her neuro team stood around like a team of footballers, all in matching uniforms—colorful bowties and white lab coats.

"Maybe it's a Harvard thing," she said to me later, having chatted them up and found out that nearly all of them were Harvard men whose daddies—and even a few granddaddies— had also been Harvard-trained neurosurgeons. "This is such a company town," she said smiling.

Eben Alexander had the easy confidence of a star quarterback. "What I like to do in these situations," he said, "is be very aggressive." He sounded like he was going to have some fun beating this little fucker into the ground. "Here's what we're going to do." Huddled around her, he called the play for the team; all she had to do was run the pattern, catch his pass, and score. The play was a new technique of targeted radiation, he said. He'd cut open her skull through the same seam, insert a radioactive implant into her brain, and leave it there for several days, while they blasted concentrated radiation directly into her frontal lobe. She would have to remain in the hospital in total isolation for the week, since she would basically be radioactive; no one would be allowed in. Nurses wearing heavily leaded HAZMAT suits would tend to her, keeping their visits in her room as brief as possible, to avoid exposure.

"I'll be a mini-Chernobyl," she said.

★ ★ ★

It seemed like that would be the hardest part to endure—having to be isolated and radioactive for a week. But as it turned out, that was the easy part. What Dr. Alexander neglected to mention was that the day before inserting the implant, the team would attach a surprisingly heavy metal stereotactic frame onto her head. This was like bolting a small oil rig onto her skull using several metal screws. Its circumference looked like the ring of Saturn, sticking out from her head by about six inches. It would serve as a frame through which the surgeons would take scans, plot trajectories, and operate on her twelve or fifteen hours later. They actually expected her to sleep overnight wearing this thing.

It was something out of the Inquisition. She couldn't lay her head against a pillow, since the combined weight of her head and the metal frame would be concentrated on just one or two of the metal bolts screwed into her skull. The pain was excruciating. But holding her head up while wearing the rig was exhausting;

she couldn't manage to do it for more than ten or fifteen minutes at a time before her neck muscles cramped.

Rafi had been with her when they'd first screwed it in, and now a few of us—siblings and friends—took turns staying up overnight with her, trying to distract her with jokes, music, and stories. We tried to hold her head up without touching the rig, and we built elaborate bridges and tunnels out of pillow and blankets in an effort to support her head and neck around it. Nothing worked, but somehow time passed.

The next morning they wheeled her off to surgery. I returned that afternoon to find her behind heavy sealed doors on the fourth floor. Giant yellow warning signs with the classic black propellor symbol for radiation were posted on her door. CAUTION – BIOHAZARD. DO NOT ENTER. Through the window in the door, the room looked spacious and apparently empty, except for Maddie propped up in a hospital bed in the middle of it. She was awake, her skull open at the front, a large tampon-looking implant stuck in her frontal lobe, with a tube leading out of it. It looked vaguely obscene. *Run away!* Was that even her? More like a crash-test dummy in some freak show.

I opened the door and walked in, momentarily impressed by my recklessness. *Fuck it, who cares*, I thought. To my surprise, another friend I hadn't noticed was already there. He and I laughed about how we would glow in the dark after we left. I held her hand, and asked how she felt. "Fine," she said. "I'm so glad to have that headgear off, I don't even care about being radioactive."

Apparently we didn't, either. Later I wondered just how foolish we'd been to hang out at her bedside, bathing in HAZMATs. The closer you were to the implant, the more dangerous. I wanted no separation between me and Maddie. At the time, I couldn't imagine living without her anyway.

In a fictional piece she would later write:

I have always hated science fiction, I still do, even though it's my life today. Where medicine ends, which I am beginning to think is shortly after it begins, science fiction takes over.

★ ★ ★

While Maddie was still in the hospital, Rafi invited me over to hang out with him and the girls. I was surprised by the invitation—I never knew what Rafi thought of me, or whether he thought of me at all. I was still committed to my assessment of him as an asshole, but when he made overtures like this, I was disarmed. It was not exactly an invitation but a good-natured command: "Come over for dinner." "When?" "Now."

Jo had the day off, and I found Rafi in the kitchen. He was wearing a faded black Phish t-shirt, the collar stretched out to accommodate his thick neck. From the back he could pass for the Incredible Hulk. He had washed half a dozen Idaho potatoes and was cutting them into big chunks. I didn't expect to see him cooking—I had assumed he didn't bother with household tasks as a matter of principle, but in fact he seemed to know exactly what he was doing, even if his style was a bit caveman: he came down on those potatoes as if with a broadsword, cold clean whacks, definitive and deadly. The potatoes fell to pieces under his hands.

"You cook," I said. I couldn't keep the surprise out of my voice. I, myself, didn't exactly "cook," and I'd never done anything to a potato except bake it. (Baking was my preferred kitchen activity—cookies, pastry, sweet things.) I wasn't sure I would even know how to prepare potatoes as he was doing. I needed to consult a cookbook before knifing anything. Maddie was not much of a cook, either. It didn't interest her, but she managed to get the kids fed.

"Of course I cook." He didn't look up or lose his rhythm. "I had to cook in the army," he said. "I hated it." He bit the words off.

He scooped the chunks of potatoes in his paws and dumped them into a frying pan on the stove. He drizzled olive oil over them and cranked up the gas.

"In Israel, the army keeps kosher, which was so stupid, because you had to lug around two sets of pots and pans, separate dishes—it was ridiculous."

I pictured troops with pots and pans clanging, attached to their rucksacks and belts.

"As a soldier, you already have to carry around an entire apartment's worth of equipment. The only reason we won the war is because Arabs are complete idiots."

I could see Maddie rolling her eyes. She was used to his deprecation of entire swaths of the human race. He'd claimed that drug addicts lacked willpower, unemployed people were lazy, and my clients were all guilty. His smug confidence annoyed me even more than the fact that we were worlds apart politically. "Of course I'm right," he liked to say.

I was a great self-doubter; I had more than a casual relationship with self-loathing. Perhaps in the privacy of my own conflict-cluttered mind, I was just as opinionated and judgmental about the world as Rafi. The difference was, I tended to avoid confrontation. Rafi, on the other hand, enjoyed being provocative, and was happy to tell you why your ideas were wrong. Tact, he believed, was a waste of time. He delivered his pronouncements the same way he cut those potatoes. Direct, sharp, quick. No room for discussion, your arguments just fell to pieces in the pan that he had already heated under you.

At the time, I couldn't imagine how dramatically my relationship with him would change within a year.

CHAPTER 11

Spring, 1990

Maddie completed her course of intensive radiation; they removed the implant, sewed her up, and sent her home to heal. The next day, while Rafi was back at work and the kids were at school, I went to see her. She lay like a large silk scarf on the king-size bed. Sunshine filled the master bedroom with its skylit high ceilings and enough space for a small squash court. Over the past year, Maddie and I had spent countless days and evenings in this room while she recovered from surgery and radiation. It was so bright, you couldn't help but feel good here. It's where the kids hung out with her after school, where friends dropped by to visit her, and now, the day after her week in the hospital, it was where we spent the morning. Just seeing her was an instant hit of pure joy. I forgot about the cancer and radiation; my heart soared in her presence.

Of course, I was relying heavily on the twin miracles of denial and compartmentalization. My mind was divided into neat containers—one for my legal work, one for my writing, one for my parents and sister, and one for my queer life, including a palatial room for Maddie. But even in Maddie's room, I kept separate drawers—one that included cancer, and one that did not. I was able to walk into her bedroom now and somehow forget that she was dying, even as I registered the physical results of the surgery. I only saw Maddie on her bed, looking radiant, surrounded by books and sunlight. Through some trick of my mind, when I was with her, I felt only how alive she was. After I left, the cancer drawer flew open, filling me with dread of her death.

I leaned over; we kissed gently. I sat next to her on the bed and asked how she was doing.

"I've got a whopping headache."

Her face was still swollen from the steroids, and the seam across her scalp puckered with black shiny stitches. I ran my fingers lightly across her forehead to distract her from the pain. I always felt protective of her incision, as if it were my responsibility to check on it each day, to smooth out its ripples. Perhaps I was trying to ease open that cancer drawer now and see all of her at once—my beautiful lover *and* the cancer that was killing her. The incision was a sort of border that separated part of her from me, the line of entry into her mind that cancer had infiltrated, leaving me outside. I wanted to go straight to the heart of her pain without flinching; I wanted nothing to come between us.

"Are you able to read?" I asked, glancing at the stack of books rising from her nightstand.

"A little." She sighed. "I'm just so tired." She got up slowly and made her way to the bathroom. "Let's have tea," she said.

I went to the kitchen, made a pot of mint tea, and brought it back to her in bed. She propped herself up on pillows and looked out the windows. The arms of the oaks held a fresh bouquet of green leaves like a gift, a bounty.

"I can't wait to go out for a walk." She sounded like a little kid, jealous of everyone playing outside. I wondered whether she resented the gaudy health and freedom of movement I took for granted. Health is wasted on the healthy.

"Tomorrow maybe," I said. We both knew it would be days before she could make it down the three flights of stairs to the street, much less go for a walk. "When is Jo coming?" I asked, to change the subject.

"Not for hours," she said.

We had the morning to ourselves. As usual, we wound up talking about writing—about one of the stories Maddie had been working on before the radiation implant. "I've never done so much writing in my head before," she said. "It's kind of strange, but it actually works. I just need to get to my computer before I forget what I've worked out."

I couldn't imagine composing a sentence, much less a story, "in my head." I had no idea what was even *in* my head until I wrote it down. I'd once heard Grace Paley field a question from someone in the audience at a reading— "Why do you write?"— with the simple response: "To find out what I'm thinking." *Yes!* I'd thought. *Me and Grace!* As though we were the only two writers in the world who felt this.

Since then, of course, I'd learned that there are endless routes and reasons for getting words on the page. Maddie was more intentional than I: she'd come up with an idea for a story before actually writing it. I, on the other hand, usually started with an image or a cluster of words that caught my attention, throw them down on the page, and see what happened.

"I'm still haunted by that little bald-headed boy in his camo outfit," Maddie said. "Franklin. I've got to write about him." She'd seen him every week while waiting for whole-brain radiation in the hospital last year. "His mother brought his younger siblings along like little ducklings, but Franklin always looked so happy, almost beatific."

"Did you talk with them?"

She nodded. "It really snapped me out of myself," she said. "I felt lucky."

I felt lucky, too. Maddie's cancer had, in a way, given us permission to be together—we didn't have to wait for her to leave Rafi or divorce him. A time bomb had been thrown into our budding affair, and it pretty much relieved us of the usual guilt and rules of self-restraint. Perhaps that's why I never shied away from even the most gruesome aspects of her treatment—not because I was courageous, but because I was starving. I would have slipped inside that seam myself, so great was my need for intimacy, for fusion.

This existential hunger of mine was a perennial problem. Now when I was away from Maddie, I filled myself with sweet things, then swam extra miles in an effort to redeem my self-esteem, if not my waistline. That's how I lived in those days, bungee-jumping from one extreme to another. Overeat, then overexercise, over and over again.

What would happen if I just sat still? *Impossible.* In those days, if I'd been forced to "sit with my feelings," as my therapist Lisa often suggested, it would have been a hostage situation: me strapped to a chair, surrounded by jackbooted, spike-collared muscle heads with truncheons. In other words, I carried a lot of anger, most of which I kept tucked away. What snuck out was my hunger.

Only with Maddie could I be still. When I was at her side, the hours floated by on little clouds. But the minute I left her, I was flooded by the realization that she was dying and that I would lose her. Late at night, when my office, the gyms and swimming pools of the city were closed, I cried in my apartment, letting rage and grief fuel the fire in my head. I never let Maddie see me break down, and I never saw her in tears, either. She later wrote that she waited until she was alone to cry. We seemed to be alike in that regard.

"Don't go," she said now, beseeching. "Wait another half hour?" She glanced at the clock. "I'm due for my *Feeny* at 11."

We'd nicknamed the Phenobarbital she took four times a day *Feeny Barbie Doll*, *Feeny* for short. Irreverent humor was our go-to drug in fighting cancer. We wanted to be on a first-name basis with the medications that prevented seizures.

"Of course," I said, grinning. "I wouldn't want to miss that."

★ ★ ★

Obstacles have a way of sharpening desire—the less access I had to Maddie, the more acute my need. When would I get to be alone with her again? I never knew Rafi's schedule; even Rafi didn't seem to know his schedule until minutes before he found himself en route to the office or to the airport or back to the apartment.

I was so tired of living in limbo like this—Maddie's cancer was hard enough to bear, without also having to wait in the wings to see her. I could never make plans of my own. I was always on call, ready for her to phone me whenever Rafi was gone. Rafi came and went like the wind. This was just the deal I had signed on for when she got sick. And I was desperately grateful for whatever scraps of time I could get with her. But waiting for Rafi's departures forced the rest of my life on hold.

What was "the rest of my life?" Much of it was devoted to the task of not going bonkers. Every morning my alarm went off at 5:15 so I could get to the pool by 6:00 for a mile swim before work. (I had learned from an early age that if I didn't work out at least an hour a day, I would be a mental wreck.) Twice a week after swimming I went to see Lisa to shore up my mental health further. When I reached the public defender office, Anita kept me going through the rest of the day by giving me half a dozen assignments, interrupting me every few minutes with funny stories, new ideas for old assignments, and questions about what I'd gotten done so far. It was like having a really smart, really funny playmate with whom to tilt at the windmills of the criminal injustice system all day. I spent evenings and weekends reading and writing stories for the MFA program, another form of therapy. And on a moment's notice, I was ready to drop everything to see Maddie.

When Maddie first got sick, I was appalled that Rafi seemed to spend more time at work than with his wife. On the plus side, this alleviated my guilt for sleeping with her when he wasn't around. And he was almost never around. For that I have Christopher Columbus to thank. During the first two years of Maddie's illness, Rafi was working non-stop as the lead producer of an epic documentary series on Columbus, pegged to the 500th anniversary of his voyage to the Americas. Not only did Rafi research and write the script, but he also flew all over the world to film it, collaborating with international production crews. In Brazil, an exact replica of the Niña was built and Rafi filmed the crew sailing it on the open sea. He arranged interviews with experts and leaders of indigenous nations. He oversaw filming in nearly thirty countries, including Argentina, China, Cuba, Ghana, Egypt, Malaysia, Nigeria, Peru, Philippines, Turkey, and Venezuela.

While Rafi circled the globe for Columbus, Maddie was making her voyage across the stormy seas of brain cancer. Domestic medical adventure was not Rafi's strong suit. "He's not that kind of guy," she said with a sigh. "He's not a caregiver. I know that about him, it's ok."

To be honest, I'd never thought of myself as much of a caregiver, either. I had no experience helping others. As a child, I'd earned the label of "selfish" in my family, the one least likely to give a shit if someone was in need. My parents' only need was for me to show undivided loyalty to our family of four. The fact that I wanted to be with my friends was considered high treason. "You only think about yourself!" my mother shouted. "Selfish, selfish, selfish."

At sixteen, I discovered Ayn Rand's book of essays, *The Virtue of Selfishness*, and raised it in my defense. "Morality is not a contest of whims," I quoted to my mother. "I may be selfish, but Ayn Rand makes a pretty good argument that selfishness is much healthier than self-sacrifice." Mom dismissed my argument out of hand.

So it was a huge relief to find myself an undeniably devoted caregiver when Maddie got sick. I never thought of Maddie's illness as good for my self-esteem, but I certainly liked the person I turned out to be with her—much more than the person I had been in my family, or the person I was when I'd broken up with Carla. As Maddie's lover and caregiver, I had unexpected new respect for myself. It was the one area in which I felt superior to Rafi.

Were Rafi and I in competition? Well, we both wanted the same female, so we had that traditional Animal Kingdom thing going. And by the laws of the wild, I was toast. But by the laws of Love in the Time of Cancer, I was a contender. Rafi's Achilles heel was Columbus. If he was going to leave Maddie for his work, I was going to be there to take his place at home.

* * *

Then there were the kids.

When they came home from school, they ran down the hall to the bedroom, dumped their book bags on the floor and climbed on the bed, turning it into a great big lounge. To them, I was simply Mummy's best friend. Maddie and I could cuddle with them and with each other without raising suspicions of impropriety—such is the privilege of being female in a straight man's world.

Eva had just turned eleven and Rachel was almost thirteen. They chattered away, telling stories from school, talking about their teachers and classmates and what they'd done in class. Eva demonstrated cartwheels and other gymnastics moves and tumbled from the bed to the floor and jumped back onto the bed again. Rachel teased her, Eva poked her back.

I couldn't tell what the girls felt about their mother's illness—her disappearance into the hospital for days at a time, then returning to them shorn and stitched up, with less energy and more pain. Did they hide their fears from themselves or only from us? Maddie never seemed to ask them about their feelings, at least not in my presence. She was a very easy-going mother, letting them steer the direction of conversation and play.

Hanging out with them was effortless. Amazingly, there seemed to be room for all of us—something quite marvelous, something that I'd never felt in my own home growing up. At times I wondered whether I was more like the girls on that bed or more like their mother. Were the two kids performing for Maddie and me, or were the girls and I all performing for Maddie? Maybe it was a little of both. I took pleasure in making Maddie laugh, just as the kids did. And I could be physically rambunctious with them, while Maddie lay still, or propped herself up on pillows, watching us.

Which surprised me because I would have expected I'd want Maddie all to myself, that I'd resent her attention diverted by the girls. So I was relieved to find myself feeling quite the opposite—the kids deepened and multiplied the sense of intimacy and joy in the house. They made me feel part of their family, something I longed for almost as much as I longed for Maddie.

★ ★ ★

Some days her energy flagged and she was too tired to write, but she still managed to do her course work for the writing program with a few extensions of deadlines to accommodate her medical treatments. The word "deadline" took on greater significance now. She was sleeping much more these days. Her headaches got worse.

"It hurts to think," she'd say. Literally. A dagger of pain when a thought came to mind, or when she concentrated on a story or an argument or a poem. I imagined drawing a map of her thoughts, connecting the dots, tracing their shapes and soothing them. It helped when I gently massaged the seam across her head, sometimes blowing on it, sometimes drawing pictures on her scalp with my fingertips and asking her to guess what I was drawing. Sometimes I wrote words, carefully tracing out each letter across the front of her head and waiting for her to understand before continuing to the next word. It seemed to distract her and ease the pain. I wrote her love letters. I described us in our little yellow cottage by the sea.

CHAPTER 12

One weekend when Rafi was out of town, Maddie called me over to hang out with her and the girls. It was a rainy spring day, and we were bored, so Maddie proposed a fashion show. We trooped into her bedroom as she fished around in the closet for something. She brought out a large antique hat box, beautifully decorated with Victorian designs, and presented it to me.

"Don't get too excited," she said. "It's from the second-hand store on Cypress."

"Ooooooh!" The kids said, and jumped on the bed to watch.

Nestled in tissue was a beautiful white wide-brimmed felted wool hat—the sort of striking fashion statement Maddie could pull off. The girls squealed with delight.

"Wow," I said. The only hats I'd ever worn were baseball caps and ski hats.

Maddie placed it on my head, angling it first one way, then the other. She leaned back, assessing. "Yes," she said. "It's perfect."

I looked at myself in the mirrored closet doors. It *was* a beautiful hat. "I love it," I said. "I feel like a movie star! Thank you." I threw my head back dramatically, posing for a glamour shot, and wondered if I would ever have the ovarian fortitude to wear something like this in public. "It's a little outside my comfort zone," I said.

Maddie smiled. "You should do something that scares you ..."

"I know, I know," I said, laughing. "Ok, who wants to try it on?"

The girls clamored for it. Maddie went through her closets, pulling out long colorful scarves and we took turns voguing for each other. Then Maddie pulled out a bag of make-up and cosmetics—lipsticks and eyeshadow, blush and eyeliner. I was a little amazed that Maddie possessed such a plethora of this stuff. My mother had one or two lipsticks, and a small jar of some kind of powder she patted onto her cheeks when she got dressed up, but that was it. I didn't know how make-up worked. I'd always had disdain for it—I considered it phony, a crass way to look attractive to men.

But now Maddie decided it was The Hoolie Make-Up Hour. She instructed me to sit very still, hold my head up, eyes closed. The three of them—Maddie, Rachel, and Eva, all took turns dabbing my face with creams, then smoothing them in; applying something called foundation, brushing my cheeks with something powdery. I felt the softness of the brushes, the gentle feel of a crayon outlining my eyes. The feel of their breath on my cheeks.

Something was happening to my eyebrows now—then something was being rubbed in or rubbed off, I couldn't tell. The three of them kept up a lively patter.

"Wait, Mummy, try this!"

"No this! Use this!" Rachel's voice rose above her sister's.

"Loolie, stop smiling," Maddie said to me. "Keep your face relaxed."

"But it tickles!" I said, laughing.

"Shush. You just messed it up," she scolded. I felt her rubbing my checks with her finger, then applying something again with a light brush.

I felt petted, the center of attention. Like a beloved creature, perhaps a rare zoo animal, attended to by three make-up artists. Thinking back on this, it was one of the headiest feelings in my life, yet the furthest thing I'd ever wanted—to be femmed-up, turned into a fashion model. I was wearing my faded Levi's 501 jeans and college rowing t-shirt. But my face was being revamped, and after everyone had gotten their hands in on it, and after Maddie had erased and revised and touched up everything, they finally let me open my eyes and presented me with a handheld mirror.

"*Holy shit!*"

The girls danced around, gleeful. Maddie was beaming—this was girl play, something I'd never done before. I stared at myself in the mirror. From the neck up I was completely unrecognizable. I looked like a *woman*.

"Hoolie, put on the hat!" Eva said.

Staring in the mirror, I could see how they'd transformed me into someone else—some*thing* else—and I marveled at the whole idea of make-up. Of make-believe. It was fiction. Passing as a woman.

Or that's what it seemed to me—I felt like a kid, not an adult. And I certainly didn't feel particularly *womanly*. More woman than man, for sure, but something closer to *boy* than girl.

"What do you think?" Maddie asked.

"Hideous!" I said with delight.

One evening a few weeks later, I brought over some fresh-baked macadamia cookies. The girls jumped up and down with excitement. "Loolie, Loolie, Loola!" This was what I loved about baking.

We demolished half of the cookies, discussing the pros and cons of macadamia nuts versus chocolate chips. The girls said they liked white chocolate chips. I was horrified. "White chocolate is an abomination!" I said.

"We love white chocolate!" the girls sang.

"Ok, I can't even look at you right now," I said. "I'm sorry, we can't be friends. I have my principles."

"We'll make you watch us eat white chocolate!" they shrieked. "We'll lock the door! You won't be able to escape."

I lunged at them, and they danced away, laughing. "White chocolate! White chocolate!"

I held my hands to my ears, in mock agony.

Eventually the kids settled down and went back to their rooms. Maddie took me by the hand, led me into the living room, and said we needed to talk. Her fingers felt delicate in my hand. "Listen, Hools," she said when we were both seated on the sofa. Through the windows behind her, the sky glowed violet under a gibbous moon. "I've thought about this, and I want you to find a girlfriend."

"*What?*" I felt sucker-punched, unable to breathe. My mind went blank. From the kitchen, I heard the faint hum of the dishwasher.

"This isn't fair to you," she said. "You should have your own girlfriend." Her voice was calm. Irritatingly unruffled.

I stared at her, stunned. "Well it's not exactly fair to you, either," I said, sitting up. "And *you're* my girlfriend." I searched her face, trying to understand what was going on. "I don't care about sex," I said. "Is that what this is about?"

In fact, I would have wanted to have sex with her, but I had no room to think about it when she was so weak, so tired and susceptible to headaches. We hadn't made love since winter, before the radiation implant. In the past two months, as she regained her strength, we'd done nothing more than hold each other. I was prepared to live without sex for as long as she was alive.

She smiled sadly and shook her head. "Please, Hoolie, I mean it. This isn't good for you. I want you to be out doing things, meeting people, having fun."

I couldn't believe it. What she was asking was impossible. "Maddie, I don't want to do anything else. I love you. Don't you get it? I need to be here with you. I can live without sex; I can't live without you."

She closed her eyes, and I could see she was in pain. I stroked her head softly. "Are you ok?"

"This is important, Hools. You need to buy a place of your own, find a girlfriend, start your own life."

Her words upset me. This *was* my life. "What's going on?" I asked.

She said nothing and we held each other. Her head grew heavy on my shoulder.

After a while, I slipped out, wrapped myself in my wounded pride, and walked home. The street looked alien to me. The very sidewalks had turned traitorous. How could she even *think* I'd date anyone else? I wasn't about to let go of her until I was forced to. I resented her trying to release me before then. As she dwindled, I was not willing to give up even a scrap of her, not a minute, not a breath.

Then I remembered something Maddie had told me years ago: When her mother was dying of breast cancer, her father, at seventy, had found solace in a new girlfriend. When Maddie told me this, I remembered being surprised—not only that he had started a new romance—but that Maddie and her sisters had been supportive of his affair while their mother was still alive. *Was that a guy thing?* I'd wondered. It seemed inconceivable.

Looking back now, over thirty years later, it occurs to me that Maddie was trying to face death, manage her losses, and do the same for me. Just as she'd enjoyed dressing me up as a way for us to play together, she now wanted to arrange a new life for me to try on—a nice home with a fully-furnished girlfriend. As if by substituting new props, I could be happy and she could see how my life would look without her. The play would go on after she was gone; this was her last chance to play a part in my future life. Perhaps she also imagined that a nice new house and new girlfriend would help cushion the blow of her eventual death.

I think she saw this as a gift she could give me.

She kept after me about it. "You deserve a girlfriend who isn't sick," she insisted a few days later, as I sat at her bedside picking at a loose thread in the quilt.

"Yeah, and you deserve a life free from brain cancer," I said. "But here we are."

She closed her eyes. "I can't give you what you need."

"What do you mean? What do you think I need?"

"I'm a lousy girlfriend, Hools. You're young, you should be out there, going places, doing things with a real girlfriend."

"I'm thirty-two," I said. "And I don't want to go anywhere. I want to be with you. Nothing else matters."

Wait—was she *breaking up with me*? "Are you breaking up with me?" I asked.

She shook her head. "No." She sighed. "I need you too much."

"Ok, good. Because you're scaring me right now."

We seemed to be getting into a power struggle, Maddie and I: who was in control of my life? She was right—I had a lot of growing up to do. She was going to teach me something about love. And about death.

★ ★ ★

I finally gave in to house-hunting. My parents had also started urging me to get my own place; they'd just helped my sister buy a house; now it was my turn. *We won't live forever,* they said. *We want to see you settled in your own home.* They were starting to sound a bit like Maddie.

I felt grateful and guilty for my undeserved privilege. My parents had come to the States with two suitcases and $50 to their name. They'd worked day and night to lift me onto their shoulders, launch me into the world, and now help me buy a house. I was drowning in debt to them, and I knew that even as my father proudly urged his hard-earned money on me, he felt bitterly dismayed that he and my mother had raised such a spoiled American brat. (This was undeniably true, particularly in my twenties, when I left law school to work as a farmhand on a dairy farm, a Hut Girl in the Appalachian Mountain Club, and a Peace Corps Volunteer in Africa. I'd certainly failed to perform in accordance with family expectations.)

So it was with both shame and gratitude that later that spring of 1990 I went on a high-speed real estate blitz. Every Sunday I bought *The Boston Globe* and studied the real estate section. I circled all the open houses I could afford within a five-mile radius, and mapped out a route from one place to another through Allston, Brookline, and Brighton. Then I jumped in my car and dashed through a dozen open houses in a single afternoon. I still couldn't afford anything in our neighborhood, so I looked farther afield: Jamaica Plain, Mission Hill, Central Square and East Cambridge. It was obvious I was not going to be living within walking distance of Maddie. A year ago, she'd nixed a Jamaica Plain condo because it was too far away. But by now she was practically pushing me to look in other towns, knowing that I could get more house for my dollar there.

After a few weeks, I got pretty good at sizing places up before even setting foot inside; I could cross some addresses off my list just by driving by. Within a month, I'd seen forty or fifty homes for sale. And then I found it, only two miles from Maddie's: a small cottage near Central Square in Cambridge. Not yellow, and not on an ocean like our fantasy cottage, but affordable. It was like a doll house for Goldilocks—a tiny little yard, a little bedroom and bath upstairs under the eaves, a little living room that opened to a postage-stamp deck, and a baby kitchen, complete with a doll's house dishwasher that could hold about five plates and glasses. I drove Maddie over to see it, and she loved it. "This is perfect," she said. "Girls will flock to you." I didn't care about girls, I cared about her. My parents helped me with the down payment, I gave my landlord notice, and I moved in that summer.

And once again, Maddie was right. The house changed me. Now that I had an actual kitchen with a functioning fridge and stove, I invited Maddie and even Rafi and the kids over. I invited my boss Anita. Friends from work. Who knew I'd ever have so much fun *cooking*? And hanging out with friends at *my own place*?

* * *

That summer Maddie wrote a short story, "Six Months to Live: Notes for a Nasty Patient Voice." Assuming a fictional male persona, she allowed herself to say things she hadn't said out loud.

I have had my skull opened, my face folded out of the way. (Sorry, but there is no reason you should be spared. That's right, they can sort of peel the face back.) For thirty-three days I have let my brain be radiated by beams that drove the technicians into hiding. Not so bad, everyone said, and it wasn't, compared to the craniotomy. But there was something awful about volunteering—no, I mean voluntarily letting them position you, matching tattoos to laser beams ...

I know what you are thinking.

It's amazing, but ever since they scooped out that piece, I can read minds. You are thinking, he's angry, bitter at the healthy world, the world with hair, that doesn't yawn, that feels good about x-ing days off the calendar. Am I angry that you can plan for Christmas when you are stuffing yourself with Thanksgiving? That you can even contemplate SPRING? No, not really, I just feel that your stupidity is showing.

On my good days I want to provoke you to stop taking your lives for granted. On my bad days I want you to stop wasting my time with how callously you treat your own.

CHAPTER 13

July, 1990

We returned to Warren Wilson for the summer residency. As usual, we shared a cab to the airport, flew to Charlotte, switched to a prop plane for Asheville, then rented a car. Maddie's stamina was impressive. She had managed to complete her semester for the program, and was eager to spend ten days with our writing colleagues. Some of our friends who had entered the program with us had already graduated; you could fast lane it to the MFA in two years and five residencies, though many people chose to take an extra semester. Maddie and I were on the slow boat—this was already our sixth residency. We clung to our community of writers and the structure of the program like a lifeline, and now, finally, we were embarking upon our final semester. Beyond that, the open sea.

A month later, in August, while Rafi was working in Spain and the girls were away at camp, Rafi agreed to let Maddie stay with me in Cambridge for the week. I was thrilled. I scrubbed the house till it sparkled, stocked up on food, and rolled out the red carpet of my fantasies.

What was Rafi thinking? By now I imagine he saw our relationship as simply convenient—his work schedule was unrelenting, and he could concentrate on his film series without worrying about Maddie or feeling guilty about being away so much. The children had not become degenerate lesbians; our arrangement worked. He probably didn't want to know too much. He was not much for emotional exploration.

After he left for Spain on Friday, Maddie insisted on taking the T to my place herself, planning to arrive at six-thirty, after I got home from work. It would take her forty-five minutes to cross the river with a change of trains at Park Street, which she managed without a hitch. But when she emerged from the T station at Central Square a few blocks from my house, she got confused and lost her bearings. The sky a searing blue, the sun blazing. She wandered around the neighborhood, looking for my street. It didn't occur to her to find a payphone and call me. I'd already changed out of my work clothes, set out some cheese and crackers, and got worried when she was late. After about fifteen minutes, I taped a note to my front door telling her to wait there, and rushed out looking for her.

I found her a few blocks away. She seemed to be floating down the sidewalk—that magnificent posture and statuesque bearing of hers. But under her wide-brimmed hat, she wore a dazed expression on her face. I wrapped my arms around her, and she seemed surprised by my concern. "I got a little turned around is all," she said. "I'm fine." She was carrying a light shoulder bag with her toothbrush, some spare underwear. Lately she had taken to wearing long kaftans, dark batik prints—no waistline, zips or buttons. Bloated from all the steroids and medications, she couldn't be bothered with the sort of clothes she'd been so intent on having me wear the year before. Her fashion taste had come over to my side: comfort and ease first. But she could still rock a kaftan like no one else.

As we walked down my street, I could tell something was off. "Are you ok?"

She lifted her hand to her head. "It just seems so much farther away." She sounded forlorn.

I opened the door and as she entered I realized that her dress was wet: she was incontinent. "Oh you poor thing," I said, trying not to let my alarm show. "Let's get you out of those clothes."

I didn't want to acknowledge that this signified anything— that her brain was coming apart in unpredictable ways. I wanted to treat it as a one-off accident. It could happen to anyone.

But she was clearly at sea. I led her toward the bathroom. "We'll clean you up and I'll give you something to wear."

She held back, looking puzzled.

I could see she didn't understand what had happened. Awareness had shifted from her to me—not just of the immediate problem of bathing and changing her clothes, but of the fact that she was leaving me, all of us, everything. She was dying and could not be held responsible. She had become innocent.

I helped her into the tub, sponged her down, and gave her a t-shirt and a pair of sweatpants to wear. "I just got confused," she kept saying. No reason to make a fuss.

The trip across the river had worn her out. She lay on my bed and rested while I went downstairs to make supper.

Look at me, making supper. So responsible! I was trying not to freak out. Here was my dream come true: me and Maddie, the love of my life, tucked away in our little cottage, free from the straight world.

And the rude awakening: it would never be true; it would always be just a dream.

★ ★ ★

I tip-toed upstairs to see if she was ready to eat. She lay stretched out on the sheets, sound asleep. My gray sweatpants only reached her calves. I checked on her a few more times, then finally woke her at 9:00 to give her meds. "Are you hungry?" She shook her head, barely opening her eyes, then sank back into sleep.

I added her clothes to a load of laundry and stayed up to transfer them to the dryer. Then I slipped into bed beside her, careful not to wake her. I needn't have worried; she was out cold. I lay awake a long time, wondering whether I was up for this, whether I would be strong enough to help her down the stairs if she were unable to walk. How quickly she seemed to have slipped below the surface of everyday living.

★ ★ ★

The next morning I was relieved to see she was feeling much better. We snuggled. The sun scissored through the maple tree outside our window. Eventually we got up, she took her meds, washed up, and came downstairs.

She was almost too tall for the house; the cottage had been built in 1834, with fireplaces upstairs and down. The "full" bathroom was wedged under the eaves upstairs, and Maddie had to stoop to enter it. She could only stand fully upright in the exact middle of the room. The bedroom, too, was tiny; the closets were carved at an angle to accommodate the low roof. Downstairs one full wall of the kitchen consisted of the original brick oven and fireplace; several small iron doors swung open to reveal various nooks and crannies. I stored pots and pans there. Opposite the brick wall, a row of miniature modern appliances lined up: fridge, oven and stove, sink and baby dishwasher. Maddie sat on one of the stools at the little counter while I set out bagels and cream cheese.

"Feeling better?" I asked, handing her a mug of coffee.

She smiled. "I told you, you really needed a new place."

"It's not on the ocean."

"Do you have any knives?" She held the tub of cream cheese at an angle.

"Oops, sorry." I handed her a knife and watched her curl it through the cream cheese, then spread it carefully across a sesame seed bagel. So elegant.

It was Saturday. We could do anything we wanted.

"Did you bring any work?" I asked. I'd been hoping we could spend some time writing.

She threw me a bittersweet smile.

"What?"

She sighed. "I need a vacation." She sounded sad.

"We could just eat bagels all week," I suggested.

She had swallowed half her bagel in two bites, and was eyeing the others in the basket. "I'm so hungry."

★ ★ ★

We sat on the huge sofa I'd bought to replace my small plaid couch. This sofa was a piece of real estate you could get lost in. "What are you working on?" she asked, bringing her legs up and stretching out on her side. She pulled one of the pillows under her head.

"Oh God, it's a mess."

"Why? Read it to me."

We both desperately needed to carry on as usual, as if she weren't sick, as if nothing had happened. We clung to this pretense of normalcy whenever we were together. Denial was something we shared well.

I grabbed the story from my desk. It was about two teenage boys arrested for making out in their parked car. Charged with Unnatural Acts, they wind up before a trial judge who is a closeted lesbian. The story switches from the boys' fears to the judge's. Afraid to arouse suspicion of her own gay identity, the judge feels obliged to come down hard on the kids, rather than toss the case out. She wrestles with her conscience and talks about it with her partner.

"It's just a disaster," I said. "I can never make a story work when I know in advance what I want it to be about."

In fact, the story was based on a case I'd seen a few years earlier in the Boston Municipal Court, and I knew the judge through the lesbian community. I liked her, but she was a political animal, ambitious and careful not to be outed at the time. My fictionalized version allowed me to make up what the boys and the judge were thinking, but I just couldn't get it right. The story felt forced and heavy-handed.

Maddie smiled. I couldn't tell whether she'd really taken in the story, or whether her mind had drifted.

"What?" I said.

She shook her head. "Nothing." Her eyes were gentle, but she seemed to be looking past me. "It's so strange," she said. "How we complicate our lives. We make all these crazy rules and criminalize whatever scares us."

"Well, some things really *are* scary." Unlike the boys in my story, nearly all of my clients had been charged with violent offenses that qualified as undeniably criminal: rape, kidnapping, assault to murder, armed robbery, and so on.

"Of course," she said. "It's just so strange to see how far it goes. How personally threatened so many people feel about harmless things that have *nothing* to do with them."

"The law is slow," I said.

"But the law is how we're told what to be afraid of."

I'd never thought of it like that. She winced, and I could see she was in pain. "Are you ok?" I asked.

"That thought cost me," she said. "Sometimes it just hurts to think."

I touched her forehead lightly, then ran my fingers across the scar. Soon she fell asleep and I covered her with a light throw.

I tried to distract myself by working on revising my story, but I couldn't get much done. How would I take care of her if she got worse this week? I kept thinking about what she'd said—how we control our fears by making laws. And then we break the laws in order to live, to be free.

In my private kingdom, I, too, tried to control my fears by making laws. My biggest fear was losing Maddie, and the law I promulgated to control this fear: Thou shalt not need. Thou shalt be self-sufficient, independent, a person of substance. Of course I kept breaking this law because like many laws that don't work, the heart cannot be legislated.

I glanced at Maddie, the gentle rise and fall of her chest as she breathed. Loving her was illegal. Loving her was criminal in the state of Massachusetts. Then again, my crime didn't weigh very much. There were so many worse things. Cancer—now there was a *real* crime—something truly malevolent and deadly and, oh, by the way—unremorseful. Yet cancer was perfectly legal in every country on earth. It couldn't be criminalized like AIDS. (Prosecutors had tried to charge HIV-positive people at Act Up protests with crimes like Assault to Kill if they scratched or bled on cops.) Lucky cancer—not contagious, it lacked the potential for crime.

* * *

After a few hours I woke her to give her meds, and she quickly fell asleep again. I studied her face as she slept, trying to remember whether she had been this tired the week before. Just last month, when we'd planned this week together, she'd had so many ideas for what we would do together: walks along the river, to Toscanini's for ice cream, live jazz at the Green Street Grill.

Now, even when she was awake, she was too tired to go out, and it was too hot to sit in the sun on my deck. I made her iced tea, hoping to invigorate her, to spruce up our time together, as if I could author a different week for us to share. I was having as much trouble revising my story on the page as reviving her from the radioactive carpet-bombing of her brain.

For the next two days, she seemed to drift more than walk, a bewildered expression on her face. We hung out on the sofa, and between naps, we talked about our work for the writing program. She had fallen behind in her assignments, and she was starting to realize she wouldn't be able to graduate with me in January. She'd need more time to create and teach a class, as required of all graduates during their last residency. And her final thesis—a collection of stories and essays—needed some finishing touches.

As I watched her sleep, I kept adjusting my hopes and expectations from hour to hour, scaling back my idea of what our week together would be like. I discovered that it was a lot of work to take care of her now, to make sure she ate and took her medication on time, to check on her and get her whatever she needed. I finally had her to myself, but now there was less of her to have.

By the end of our second day, I had no hopes at all except to be in her presence. We were together, and that's all that mattered. Wasn't that enough? Could I get by on so little of her?

* * *

Maddie had been with me less than four days when Rafi called to say he was cutting his trip to Spain short; he'd hit a rough patch in the project, and wanted to come home for some

TLC. Maddie and I were suddenly jolted out of our fantasy of playing house together and back into the reality that Rafi was her husband, and his schedule—unpredictable as always—ran not only her life, but mine as well.

I drove her home. Jo had the week off, so I stayed with Maddie until he arrived. When he came in the door, Maddie's face beamed with happiness to see him. She held his blocky head in her long thin hands, and I felt a stab of jealousy. I hid my feelings behind a smile, welcomed him home, then grabbed my backpack and let myself out the door.

★ ★ ★

Even now, over thirty years later, I'm still ashamed of myself—my neediness—during that time of my life. It seems like evidence of mental weakness, of abysmal low self-esteem, of settling for scraps, of a failure to take care of myself, a failure to grow up. I was a contestant for the Emotionally Famished Award.

But perhaps from this vantage point, the wobbly perch of my sixties, I can cut myself some slack, simply because I was so clueless as to what love even *meant* back then. Love had always been so confusing in my family. Ours was a high-decibel, weaponized version of love, with so much passion and violence, it left no room for reflection. I never doubted my parents' love for me. But it took me a long time—decades—to realize that their love required that I be someone other than who I was. I impersonated the daughter they needed, until I couldn't, and when I couldn't, my failure came as a shocking betrayal—both to them and to me.

Maddie actually seemed to see me and love me for who I was at a time when I, myself, didn't even know who I was. This feeling of being seen and nevertheless loved was so new and so necessary, I would hang on to her as long as I could, whatever the cost.

And the cost was great. But it was still a bargain. She opened my eyes to the possibility that I could stop pretending to be the person my family needed me to be. To begin finding out who I really am.

CHAPTER 14

Fall, 1990

As if Maddie had arranged it herself, I received a call out of the blue later that fall. It was Skye Tarandon, one of the women from that Professional Women's Group hike to Lonesome Lake a year and a half ago. I didn't remember exchanging numbers; maybe she looked me up in the phonebook. It had been so long ago. I assumed she'd exhausted all the other possibilities the hike had offered, and I was her last resort.

She invited me to work out at her gym on a guest pass; afterwards she'd make us dinner. I'd never been to the Mount Auburn Club, a swank all-inclusive fitness center, complete with indoor tennis courts, Olympic sized swimming pool, sauna, hot tub, weights, juice bar, etc. It was outside my price range. "Sure," I said.

★ ★ ★

We met at the Club on a Friday night, and I was amazed to receive a plush towel and key to a private locker when we checked in. The place was palatial. Skye and I had agreed to go swimming—she was a triathlete, and I was an obsessive swimmer, so we were well matched. Afterwards we hung out in the hot tub, showered, and dressed. I was surprised by her shyness in the locker room—she wrapped herself tightly in a towel from armpit to knees, and dropped her eyes so as not to look at me. At my Boys and Girls Club in Allston, I was accustomed to swimming during the women-only early morning hours; everyone swam naked, showered together, and got dressed in the locker room in plain view.

After Skye and I dressed, I got in my Ford Escort and followed her Subaru XT sportscar to her apartment in Arlington. Her place was small but airy, furnished like a beach house.

She grabbed two beers from the fridge, popped the caps, and offered me one. We sat in her living room and talked about our work, ourselves, our past girlfriends.

"So what's your deal?" she said.

It was strange to hear myself describe my life right now; I never talked about Maddie except with my therapist.

"Well, it's kind of a mess," I said. "I'm in love with a woman who's married, has two kids, and is dying of brain cancer."

"Oh, wow. I'm sorry." She looked solemn.

"Yeah." I shrugged. "It's not ideal." I was embarrassed to admit I'd spent the last year and a half of my life like this. Maddie was right: it wasn't healthy. Describing my situation to a stranger made me realize how much shame I'd wrapped around this secret of mine.

But Skye was nice about it. She didn't pry, just expressed sympathy. I noted a trace of a southern accent in her voice—she was from North Carolina, but her diphthongs apparently had been dry-cleaned by her Ivy League education. A few years younger and a few inches shorter than I, she was an environmental scientist with the Charles River Watershed Association. Smart, funny, boyishly attractive, and uncomplicated. In fact, she was so well-adjusted and fundamentally happy, it would start to grate on my nerves after a while. I felt like a morose sepia-toned character lurking around the edges of her sunny disposition.

She was no stranger to heartache, of course—she'd lost her mother a few years earlier, and was now recovering from the breakup of a long-term relationship with her girlfriend. But her attitude toward loss seemed much healthier than mine. She was basically upbeat, energetic. She moved forward with her life, eager for tomorrow. Me, I was pretty sure the future would only kick my ass.

That evening after our swim, she asked me to stay.

"I'm sorry." I said, shaking my head. "I just ... I'm not ready." I wondered if I would ever be ready.

"Oh, lighten up," she teased, and tried to cajole me into bed. "We don't have to do anything. We can just sleep together."

At last I gave in, but I kept my shirt and underwear on. And my knee socks, for which she ridiculed me, but for whatever reason, they made me feel safe and untouchable. Amazingly, I was able to fall sleep next to her. I left the next morning before dawn and drove home.

★ ★ ★

What's she like? Maddie wanted to know.

I shrugged. *She's young*, which was rich, coming from me, a case study in delayed emotional development. She was twenty-nine.

Physically, she was the opposite of Maddie in every way. A sparkplug of solid muscle, blue-eyed, fair-haired. Her sense of humor was refreshingly low-brow. Or was it annoyingly low-brow? It depended on my mood.

"Hools, this is good for you," Maddie said. "I'm really happy for you."

I was not happy. It was creepy, having the love of my life encourage me to get a girlfriend.

"You need to get out there," Maddie said. "Have fun."

Telling a depressive to have fun doesn't work. "I love *you*," I said.

She sighed. "So think of it as an assignment."

* * *

Skye was, in fact, good company. Well-read, clever, and funny. We both loved the outdoors, and spent a weekend scrambling up and down trails in the White Mountains. Later that winter we went cross-country skiing in Franconia. She was fun to be with, and as it turned out, she was fun in bed, but part of me was missing; I coasted along the surface, going through the motions. She took me to parties at her friends' penthouse apartments in the Back Bay and South End, where wine and whiskey flowed, lines of coke were discreetly available, and hairstyles and outfits were stacked high and wild, but I felt like a spectator—a dud, a one-beer-and-done girl. Skye, on the other hand, was the life of the party. I stood on the sidelines, the gap between us widening.

I would go over to see Maddie after work sometimes and on weekends, but talking about our writing seemed to drain her. Her headaches could stop her mid-sentence. I traced the line of her scar with my fingertips as usual, and saw a faint smile form on her lips. But abruptly she opened her eyes.

How's Skye?

I'm trying, I said. There was nothing wrong with Skye.

You won't want to come here anymore. She sounded pitiful.

I shook my head. *If I could, I'd be here all the time.* But was that really true? I worried that my devotion was flagging. It was hard to keep turning my schedule upside down to be with Maddie, only to find her asleep much of the time. She was unable to talk for long before lapsing into headache-induced silence. My amorphous role of girlfriend/best friend weighed on me— how exactly did I fit into her life now?

I couldn't tell what my therapist Lisa thought about my affair with Skye. I sensed her disapproval, which is to say, I sensed *my* disapproval. I felt guilty about seeing Skye while pining for Maddie. My problem with Skye was that she was just way too happy.

★ ★ ★

January 1991: it was our seventh residency. On the last day, I would graduate from the writing program and Maddie would not. She now planned to graduate in July.

As always, I hovered close to her, walked her to and from classes, and brought her food. She didn't bother going to the cafeteria at all anymore, and for the first time, she was too tired to go to many classes. As her body grew heavier and more solid, her mind became ethereal, turning more and more into air. She managed to participate fully in the morning workshops, but then returned to her room. She slept through many of the afternoon classes, emerging in the evening for the readings.

I, on the other hand, like the eight other graduating students, was busier than usual: I had to teach my class and give a reading, in addition to the regular workload. It drove home the fact that Maddie's and my paths were diverging; I was moving forward, and she was being held back. I gave my graduate reading one evening, while Maddie sat in the front row, smiling, her black patterned kaftan draped along the length of her. On the last night, the other graduates and I received our diplomas. Once again she sat in the front and beamed. It broke my heart.

★ ★ ★

A couple of months after the residency, Maddie went in for her regular checkup and MRI. It was late February, two years after her diagnosis, and the news was not good. The tumor had come back; it was now half the size of the neurosurgeon's thumb—Eben Alexander held up his thumb to show us. He had his assistant schedule surgery as soon as possible, then jumped to his feet with a flourish. *We'll nip it in the bud*, he said, and sailed out of the office.

Rafi was at her side when we got the news. Maddie seemed calm. Perhaps we all seemed calm. We tucked this thumbprint of information into our denial hardware, and went home to clear our calendars.

Very early the morning of surgery, Rafi drove her to the hospital. It was still dark; the streets were empty. As they crossed the Muddy River she looked at him and said, *Let's not go. Let's run away.* She told me this a few hours later, as she and I sat in her hospital room after they'd drilled the stereotactic frame into her head. Blood crusted around the screws in her skull. Once again, the horror-show look.

It was another hour or two before they finally wheeled her off to surgery. This was her third brain operation, and we were getting used to the deal: handing her over to the surgeons, receiving her back a day later, diminished. I felt relief that soon she would be free of the metal frame, and free of the new tumor.

After seeing her off, I took myself and my anxiety to my office to get some work done. It was a good distraction, but unlike Rafi, I couldn't entirely lose myself in work. Maybe Rafi couldn't either; we were all just doing our best to get by. My boss Anita was a lifesaver. *Do whatever you need to do*, she said. I'd repeat her words to myself like a mantra. Another piece of advice from her: *You do not have to do the hardest thing.* This came as a welcome shock: I'd always considered it my obligation to do the hardest thing, confusing hardship with strength. My self-esteem was somehow dependent on suffering. After all, my parents had done *the hardest thing*—they'd experienced unspeakable horror, and had somehow survived. My privileged life rendered me unworthy, a subsidiary being.

Anita helped me get over myself. And at the same time, she offered clear-eyed compassion and a hefty dose of badass humor. Boss and guru in one.

Dr. Alexander called Rafi that evening to tell him the surgery had gone well; he'd removed the tumor, and Maddie would be back on her feet in no time. Now Alexander was heading off to Aspen for a ski vacation with his family. "All clear," Rafi said when he called to let me know. I thanked him for the news and went to bed.

Rafi's next call woke me up at midnight. Maddie had started hemorrhaging, and was taken back in for emergency surgery. "Meet me at the Brigham," he said. I raced across town, parked on the street, and ran to the neuro floor. Rafi was already there. The hospital was quiet, empty.

"Any word?" I asked. He shook his head.

We waited, each wrapped in our own thoughts. Occasionally he or I walked up and down the long hallway, unable to sit still. I was grateful for his presence; it would have been much harder to do this alone. Maybe he needed me here, too—after all, he'd called me of his own accord. I wanted so badly to be part of Maddie's family. It was a little pathetic, how much I wanted that validation—to be recognized as someone who legitimately loved her, someone equally preoccupied with her well-being as a spouse or sister. The word *legitimate* haunted me. It was the one qualifier I lacked in our relationship. Instead, our love affair was *secret*—whether known, acknowledged, or denied by others—and therefore invalid. No matter what, it was categorically *illegitimate*.

And so, I felt, was I.

It was after three in the morning when a lone figure in blue scrubs slowly approached from down the hall. He looked utterly exhausted. Youngish, thin, with dark hair that sprang out in all directions. Rafi and I both jumped to our feet and rushed toward him.

"Madeline Brinley?" he said.

We nodded.

"I'm Dr. Mars."

You could see he needed sleep. He needed a shave.

"How is she?" Rafi asked.

"She's stable now. We drained the blood in her cranial cavity and she's in recovery."

"Will she be all right?" Rafi asked.

Dr. Mars tilted his head and raised an eyebrow. "You know she has end-stage cancer, right? She's going to die from this."

His words fell like blows. Of course we knew, but part of us didn't. Neither Rafi nor I could speak.

"Sorry." The doctor shrugged, already turning and walking away.

What an asshole, I thought. My face grew hot with anger.

I looked at Rafi and saw that he had tears in his eyes.

"Are you ok?" I asked.

He nodded.

"It's all right," I said. "She's going to be ok. When do you want to visit her?"

"I'll come tomorrow before work. But I need to leave by 7:30."

I nodded. "I'll come after my swim."

I waited till I got home to cry. I always felt self-conscious around Rafi—the whole situation was awkward, and I tried my best to stay out of his way, to defer to him, to let him decide what he wanted to do, and then I'd figure out how to fit in around the edges. There was something both shameful and infuriating about my role, but it was the only role available to me.

These were the terms on which Maddie's and my relationship had been based once she'd gotten sick.

* * *

It would take me a while to forgive Dr. Mars. I felt bruised by the bluntness of his words. But later I realized that he'd probably spent the last twenty or thirty hours cleaning up the messes left by the attendings—leading neurosurgeons like Dr. Alexander—who had done their work, taken off, and left the younger doctors to deal with the consequences. After all, Dr. Mars had saved Maddie's life that night. Perhaps he was not only wiped out, but also demoralized, knowing there wasn't much of her life left to save. And annoyed that we were too stupid to see this.

CHAPTER 15

In the months before Maddie's relapse, I'd been skirmishing with Lisa over trivial things. Whatever she said (little of which I remembered) bugged me. She was just another straight woman, insensitive to my delicate lesbian gestalt. I even questioned her qualifications as a feminist (I felt dissed by some remark she'd made about a t-shirt I'd worn to therapy: "A Woman Without A Man Is Like A Fish Without A Bicycle" —an adage written by Australian social activist Irina Dunn and later popularized by the feminist Gloria Steinem.) I don't remember what Lisa's comment was, but I objected to her disparaging tone. She objected to my objection and suggested we talk about my anger. Nothing made me angrier than her suggestion that I was angry.

I'd also argued with her about what to do with a new piece of artwork that my family had brought as a house-warming present for my cottage: a framed silver bas-relief by a now world-famous Italian sculptor whom my mother had helped during the war. His beautiful sketches of female nudes hung in the living room of my parents' house.

But when my mother proudly unwrapped this shiny new bas-relief and held it up over my fireplace, I thought I would gag. Not only because it was flat-out hideous, but because of its subject. Entitled "The Kiss," it was a close-up of two faces—a stubble-bearded man (like Rafi!) kissing a woman.

No.

My jaw dropped and my mother saw that the piece was not a hit.

"You'll get used to it," she assured me.

This was one of the problems with not coming out to your parents. I was pathologically attached to them, but we never discussed my love life. Consequently:

1. They never suspected I might be queer.
2. They didn't know I'd dated or fallen in love with women. They'd never heard of Carla.
3. They knew I'd had boyfriends years ago, in college and law school. They assumed that one day I'd marry a man, but my mother frankly preferred that I stay single. She viewed any love interest as a threat to my fundamental role as daughter and sister.
4. They knew Maddie was my best friend.
5. They didn't know she was my lover.

★ ★ ★

"Why don't you just tell them you don't like the bas-relief, and give it back to them?" Lisa asked.

I looked at her as if she'd suggested I join the Hitler Youth. "Are you kidding?"

She shrugged.

"Have you heard *anything* I've told you about my family for the last seven years?"

And so on.

★ ★ ★

Now that Maddie had nearly died, I finally stopped dicking around and started *listening* to my therapist. I couldn't even talk about death in those days. I had no intimate experience with it—all my relatives had been killed before I was born, and my handful of dead friends had died in distant cities. Lisa,

I discovered, was formidable in the face of grief and loss and trauma and death. She didn't push, she didn't lead, she listened. Sometimes we just listened to each other listen to each other.

One of her greatest gifts was teaching me how to pay attention to what I was feeling. This took work. I had spent most of my life perfecting the art of avoiding any inconvenient emotions—a strategy that had enabled me to remain close to my family. The problem was, it had dangerous side-effects: my identity was slippery. Lisa was teaching me to pay attention, to trust myself, to be exactly who and where I was.

"Have you ever talked with Maddie about dying?" she asked one day.

I shook my head.

"What are you feeling?"

What *was* I feeling? "Nothing," I said.

She waited a moment, then offered, "Are you scared?"

I shook my head slowly. "No, I just ... Maybe."

"Are you afraid of her dying?"

"I mean, I know she'll die. But I don't think I can bring it up with her."

Lisa nodded. "Why is that?"

"It seems cruel. Maybe she doesn't want to talk about it. I think I have to wait for her to bring it up."

"And if she doesn't?"

"Then I have to respect that."

After her relapse, Maddie never brought up the subject of death with me. I don't know what she felt about it. Later I would regret my reticence.

★ ★ ★

The top of her head was wrapped like a mummy the morning after Dr. Mars's emergency surgery. Rafi was sitting at her bedside when I came in. I could see that he hadn't gotten any more sleep than I.

"Hey," I said to Maddie, leaning over her.

She blinked.

"How are you feeling?"

She was groggy and couldn't talk, but she seemed glad to see me.

"They say it will be a few days," Rafi said. He smiled at her. "I have to go now."

I had been relieved to see him here—Maddie needed his support—but now I was also happy to see him go. I wanted to be alone with Maddie. I could never relax when Rafi was around—our feelings were complicated and went unspoken. I knew that the first episode of his Columbus film series would air six months from now. I was glad he had work to attend to, leaving more time for me with Maddie.

I sat with her for an hour, holding her hand, telling her what had happened, assuring her that now it was just a matter of recovering and getting stronger every day. As if I knew shit. Where did this calm optimism come from? I'd always been a devout pessimist, yet throughout Maddie's illness, confident assurances of pure wishful thinking flowed from my mouth like soap bubbles. I suppose my denial was more formidable even than my depression. Maddie seemed to drift in and out of sleep, and I wasn't sure how much she took in.

Over the next few days it became apparent that the bleed in her brain and back-to-back surgeries had been devastating. She recognized us, but she'd lost the ability to walk and talk; it would be a long hard road of rehabilitation. They sent her to the Spaulding Rehab Center, a ten-minute walk from my office downtown.

I visited her every morning after my swim and before work, taking the T from Central Square to Charles Street, then walked past the jail where I used to visit my clients. I came again on my lunch break, walking across the Boston Common toward the harbor. She always broke out in a wide grin when I came in the door, and I felt nothing but elation to see her smile. I'd rush to her side, kiss her cheek, and sit on her bed, holding her hand and grinning like an idiot. Rafi preferred to visit after work, so we divided up the days like that. Weekends I spent the mornings with her, sometimes the afternoons; Rafi came in the evening. And of course, others came to visit—friends and family, spelling us from time to time.

★ ★ ★

In February, the month before Maddie's doctors had discovered the new tumor, Skye would scoop me up in her sportscar and whisk me off on various weekend adventures. She was always cooking up things to do, places to explore, parties to go to. She could have generated enough energy to operate a small town. I went along like a hopeful applicant—maybe I could fit the job description of her girlfriend? We had so much in common.

No, we were nothing alike. Skye was in love with life while I was simply in denial of death.

We visited friends of hers who owned a house near a salt marsh and walked along the mud flats. I lost interest once we went inside and started drinking. A few weeks later we spent a windy weekend in Provincetown, shacked up in an apartment she'd found through a friend of a friend. The town was deserted, cold, beautifully monochromatic.

I realized that I liked Skye better without her friends. But she obviously adored them. What did she see in me?

She saw that my mind was elsewhere. "You're still in love with her, aren't you?" she said one evening in March when I was at her apartment. A note of wonder in her voice.

Her words seemed to surprise both of us. I burst into tears.

"It's ok," she said, leaning forward and touching my arm. Her voice was so kind, I was afraid I would never stop crying. She looked at me with thoughtful, sympathetic eyes. I could see in her face the truth sinking in, the realization that although I never talked about Maddie, and although the situation was completely hopeless, Maddie was still my world.

I was grateful not to have to explain myself—I couldn't—I had no words. I shook my head. "I'm sorry."

It's ok, she repeated softly.

Perhaps I finally made sense to her.

A wave of relief rippled through me. I could stop trying so hard to be *fun*. Stop trying to keep up with Skye. She was gentle as she helped me into my jacket. Then she drove me home and told me to take care of myself and we never saw each other again.

CHAPTER 16

At first she just managed to whisper a few words and gesture with her long, graceful hands. They couldn't figure out why she couldn't speak. Nothing was wrong with her larynx, and she had no trouble understanding us. Speech therapists worked with her daily, teaching her to push air through her vocal cords. Over time, she gradually recovered her ability to speak, though her voice remained wispy, uncertain.

She now wore a blank expression on her face, but she was determined to recover and get back home. Her occupational therapist came in and made a daily schedule on a whiteboard, blocking off hourly therapy appointments—speech, physical therapy, cognitive therapy, etc. She had Maddie study the chart, look at the clock on the wall, and tell her what was on her schedule for that hour. I watched Maddie concentrate on the task, and although it took her a few moments, she gave the right answer. Then she closed her eyes, worn out.

The half dozen therapists who rotated through her room every day were all young, smart, energetic, and—as it turned out—female. They worked their butts off, and they pushed Maddie to do the same. They were also unfailingly kind, funny, and encouraging. I was completely smitten. Was it too late for me to become an occupational therapist? I looked up the requirements and realized I would never make it: a long, grueling academic program, followed by a ton of hard work, state licensure and more work. I imagined the burnout rate could be high. You didn't see any gray-haired rehab workers here.

Speech and cognitive therapists came in with flash cards and number games and encouraged me to participate. I was always unnerved to see how lousy my short-term memory was. Maddie jumped through these cognitive hoops like a gazelle. Learning to walk again was harder. In the beginning, it took the whole session just to get her to sit up, swing her legs over the side of the bed and gingerly put some weight on her feet, supported by me on one side and the therapist on the other. We practiced that for days. It was exhausting, physically and mentally. Afterwards, Maddie would sink back into bed and close her eyes, winded.

I remembered the conversation Dr. Black had had with her two years earlier, before her first operation: *would you rather lose speech or movement?*

After I'd gotten my MFA that January, I stopped writing altogether, except in my journal. As if by graduating, I'd finally earned the right to be silent. I had no energy for anything anymore but swimming, keeping my day job, and visiting Maddie, which always raised my spirits.

Once she regained some balance, we'd put her in a wheelchair and I'd take her for a ride down the hall to the bank of windows overlooking the lower basin of the Charles River. The view of the water from above was calming, and we could see bits of green poking through the gray landscape as March turned to April. The light grew softer over the next few weeks as Maddie's strength improved.

She was clearly on the upswing, improving day by day and week by week. I could almost forget she had cancer—she wasn't dying, she was recovering! Before they'd release her, she had to be able to walk with a walker, climb stairs, cook on a stove, and take care of her own activities of daily living. How hard could that be? I, a world-class worrier, had now miraculously erased Dr. Mars's words from my mind—*She's going to die from this.*

By May Maddie was able to use a walker with tennis ball feet that she could push forward a foot or two, and then inch along behind it, taking small, mincing steps. As she got stronger, we went for longer, faster walks, twenty yards down the hall and back. But she couldn't seem to make the pivot to get back into her room. She'd keep walking right past her door, turning her head and craning her neck to keep her eyes on the door as she went by. She just couldn't get her feet to turn. *Perseveration*, the physical therapist told me.

I, too, was perseverating, walking my conscious mind right down the hall of my imagination to a full recovery, unable to steer my thoughts through any door leading to her death. I stayed very much in the moment—I was about as present as I've ever been in my life—focused on each task, cheering each minor miracle of success: when she was able to do long division, for example, when she was able to shuffle to the bathroom alone with her walker, walk up her first flight of stairs. I didn't let my mind go through any other door. She was forty-three years old and steaming back into shape. Soon she would be soaring out of rehab, and heading home.

★ ★ ★

In the midst of her stunning return to life, it was disconcerting to stumble upon discrete bombed-out bridges in her brain. One day, her OT handed her a thick phonebook and asked her to look up some random name—John Smith.

Maddie easily opened the book and paged through it, concentrating. She knew the alphabet. She spoke in full sentences, could spell complicated words forwards and backwards. But this task—trying to figure out how to locate a name in a list of thousands of alphabetically arranged names—was beyond her. She knew the task was simple. She brushed off the therapist who tried to give hints—"I know how to do this," Maddie said confidently, turning another few pages, running her eyes up and down the rows of names and numbers in tiny print.

"Look up here," the OT suggested, pointing to the large-print headers at the top of the page: "Matthews – McConnell."

Maddie looked at the header blankly.

"This whole page of names all start with the letter *M*," the OT said. "So, what does—"

"I know!" Maddie's frustration was growing.

The therapist let her work on the problem a little longer. "It's ok," she finally said. "We'll come back to this. I have something else I want you to do first." She gently took the phonebook from Maddie and handed her a card with a dozen words on it, segueing to a simpler task.

After the OT left, Maddie was still annoyed. "I know how to use a phonebook," she said. "I just needed a little more time."

I agreed, shrugged it off, but inside, my heart was caving. Her inability to recall how to sequence the task didn't bother me; it was her frustration, her awareness of her disability, that I found gut-wrenching. She had recovered enough cognitive ability to inhabit the city in which she had functioned all her life; she just couldn't fathom how to get from one street to another.

Where did my anger go? While Maddie was in rehab, I felt nothing but overlapping waves of hope and sadness.

Lisa was interested in my anger; I was not. I'd spent my whole life trying to get rid of it. Now that it had magically disappeared, she wanted to go poking around to see how it was doing.

"Don't you think it's interesting ..." she began.

"No."

She laughed. "Ok, but let's think about it. A few months ago you were pretty angry at me. What's changed? Where did it go?"

I shrugged. "I saw the error of my ways." I loved Lisa, but she was always trying to stir up trouble. "I got over it."

"Well," she said in that solemn tone she reserved for revelations, "I think you got depressed instead."

"I'm not depressed."

She said nothing, just kept her eyes leveled at me.

"So I traded in my anger for depression?"

She nodded. "Something like that."

She was right. I *had* gotten depressed. Was that such a bad deal? True, I hadn't written a word since I'd graduated from the program in January. But who cared? At the moment, I felt neither angry nor depressed; Maddie's relapse had jolted me out of all that. Now I was energized, focusing on her daily improvements. Maddie's rehab was the best thing that had ever happened to me.

"That's not how it works," Lisa said. "Anger doesn't just go away."

We discussed the possible flight patterns of anger.

"I think you're angry at Maddie," she said.

I rolled my eyes. Nothing could be further from my mind.

"She's leaving you."

"She's not gone yet," I reminded her. "She's getting better every day."

Lisa nodded. "She's the one who got cancer in the first place."

"Right," I said. "Her bad."

Lisa smiled. "There it is," she said, proudly. She'd managed to find a spark of anger. My turn to laugh.

* * *

We did that for a while—dancing around the subject, trying to get me to realize how maddening the whole Maddie affair had been from the beginning. We would dosey doe up to the edge of my anger, talk about it a bit, then move on. It was easier to be angry at the doctors, at Eben Alexander for his cocky self-assurance, his ski trip to Aspen while Maddie bled through several layers of brain cells.

It seemed wrong to be angry at Maddie. Like kicking someone when she was down.

"It's not right or wrong," Lisa said. "Anger is a feeling. It just is."

Wasn't that the whole point of having a frontal lobe in the first place? To control those feelings? My frontal lobe was still intact. Why was Lisa trying to break through it?

"It takes a lot of energy to keep your anger in check," she said. "You could free up some of that energy for other stuff. Like writing, seeing friends, whatever."

I pictured my anger sitting in a cage inside my frontal lobe, hands gripping the bars. I pictured letting the door swing open … to what? I lacked either the imagination or courage to set it free.

* * *

They were going to release her. Less than three months ago she'd been at death's door, and over the past week, she'd flown through all the hoops: she could get herself to the bathroom with her walker, use the toilet, wash her face, take a bath; she managed to walk up three flights of stairs; she could open cabinet doors in the rehab kitchenette, get out a pot, boil water on the stove. She was euphoric. We were euphoric. She was going home!

It was mid-May, and the city seemed to be celebrating, trees bursting into blossom, tulips and daffodils and lilies ablaze. Goslings waddled single file behind their parents on the Esplanade; the long winter was over, and we'd won.

I got permission from the rehab staff to throw a party for Maddie in the common area on her floor the Sunday before her release on May 19. I decided to make it a Calypso Dance Party: bright colors, tropical breezes, good vibes. I invited Rafi and Chase and all of Maddie's friends I could think of. I made posters in hot pink and a rainbow of Caribbean colors announcing the event, and posted them around the hospital, inviting everyone to drop in on Sunday afternoon. I printed out multiple copies of limericks I'd written celebrating each of Maddie's team of therapists, nurses and staff, and passed them around. A Trinidadian friend in my office had his own steel drum band; I couldn't afford to hire them, so I bought a few of their cassettes to play on my boom box. I filled the trunk of my Ford Escort with bags of chips, crackers, salsa, dips, cheeses, cookies, and fresh fruit. Gallons of juice and ginger ale, bags of ice for a huge bowl of fruit punch. I'd bought cheap serving bowls and platters, party decorations. I was on fire.

It amazes me now to remember myself then, filled with excitement, imagining ... what? That she would live forever? Was I delusional? I couldn't think about forever; forever was this moment. I was overflowing with excitement, wanting to shout from the rooftops, mark this victory. She was coming home!

It was a glorious sunny day. I sped down Storrow Drive, parked at the hospital, hauled everything to her floor, and set up the party. Steel drums on the boombox, food and drinks on the long tables, streamers strung across the room. Hospital staff came from various departments, sensing the desperation of my need. I handed out party hats and noisemakers. A few of the patients on the floor even shuffled in. We turned off the lights and let the sun filter in through the windows. Once the party was rolling, I went to Maddie's room and brought her down the hall. We could already hear the music, see the signs I'd taped to the walls pointing the way.

Even with her face puffy from steroids, when she entered the room, she broke into a big smile. Our eyes met, and my heart soared. I felt I was floating, held aloft in a warm glow. We moved together in that glow, felt its embrace, and the rest of the world fell away. Maybe love is just a quality of being seen, feeling the light in someone's gaze, a connection between what's hidden within you to what's hidden within them. The underground tunnel each of us digs in solitude from our little prison cells, and when we finally break through, when the passage between us connects somewhere deep underground, we light up. Our five senses are slouches compared to this. Sight, smell, sound, taste, touch—just tools we use to gain access to this sixth sense—a broad expanse of grace that lies beyond these pedestrian feelings—the sense that you matter, that your *matter* is of central importance to the beloved. We were in our own world. *Whatever else happens*, I thought, *this moment is worth it*. I actually believed that. She beamed with pleasure. I beamed with pleasure. I asked her to dance. We set aside her walker, and she wrapped her arms around me, and we slow-danced to the calypso beat, dreamy smiles on our faces.

CHAPTER 17

Something had shifted between Rafi and me over the past few months—ever since that night in February when Maddie had hemorrhaged and they'd rushed her in for emergency surgery. He'd called me in the middle of the night, and we'd waited together at the hospital for Dr. Mars to tell us she was alive, and that she would surely die. We never spoke of the change in our relationship—Rafi was not one to talk about feelings, and I was always so self-conscious around him, I couldn't say anything, either. But his eyes had become gentler to me since that night. Every so often when we saw each other now, his boulder of a head cracked open with a smile, and his eyes lit up with kindness, and sometimes he even touched my shoulder as we took turns at her bedside, his big bear paw on my arm like the blessing of a tamed beast. I began to see the attraction of this big brute of a man once he let down the gruff exterior and his eye twinkled with sweetness or mischief or both. What I had resented before was his cold indifference; what melted me was his warmth that came quite unexpectedly like a blast from a furnace I'd assumed wasn't working.

Rafi brought her home from the hospital and called me the next day to come over. He had wrenched his back trying to lift her when she'd fallen just a few feet from the bed. I was stunned. It was inconceivable to me that Rafi, a veritable mountain of muscle, could be injured lifting Maddie. I rushed over and found him sitting on the edge of the bed, imploring her to wait for me.

"This is bullshit," she said.

Rafi and I exchanged looks. I had never seen them argue before.

"Your balance is off," he pleaded. "You don't realize it."

"So you're going to chain me to the bed?"

"You just fell down walking to the bathroom." He glanced up at me. I could see he was in pain; he sat stiffly, wincing.

"Oh Jesus! So I missed a step. Big deal! You can't keep me from moving around in my own house."

"I don't want you to get hurt."

"I won't get hurt!" She sounded like a petulant teenager. It was strange to see her like this. It reminded me of the argument we'd had a year ago, when she'd called me at work to say she was going to drive to her therapy appointment. In the end she'd done what she wanted and nothing had happened. But things were different now. She was no longer fighting for her freedom to drive across town, she simply wanted to be able to walk across the room. Her autonomy had been crushed.

"I have to go to the office," he said. "Hoolie, can you stay with her?"

"Of course." It was the first time he'd ever called me Hoolie—a nickname coined by Maddie and the kids—and I was disarmed to hear this endearment from his lips; with one word, he had stepped inside our circle of intimacy. I was happy to relieve Rafi, but also nervous. If Rafi couldn't lift her without hurting himself, how would I manage? It was obvious she was not going to stay in bed.

Rafi eased himself up and limped to the door.

"You should ice that," I said.

"You have my number at work," he said. "Call me."

"Let's go up to the roof." She sounded relieved once he left. "The plants must be miserable."

"Don't worry. I'll water them."

She swung her legs over the side of the bed. "I want to see."

I helped her up, but as soon as she was on her feet, she listed sideways and fell back onto the bed. She sat a moment, trying to understand what had just happened. Then she thrust herself up again and I caught her in my arms.

"Easy," I said, trying to steady her. We stood together swaying, arms around each other. She took a few jerky steps, but I had to hold her to keep her from falling. At last she fell back onto the bed.

"Maybe we can try a little later," I suggested.

She didn't seem to hear me. "I have to figure out what to wear to Rachel's play tonight. I have to get up."

Even while in rehab, she'd been lobbying for weeks to attend Rachel's school play. Rachel had a lead part, and Maddie was determined to be there.

"I don't think you're going to be able to go," I said as gently as I could.

She cut her eyes at me. "There's no way I'm missing her play."

For once I was relieved that Rafi would be back tonight to deal with it.

★ ★ ★

In the end it took all of us—me, Rafi, Chase, even Jo—to convince her she couldn't go to the performance. She burst into tears. I think she finally realized that it was her body that had betrayed her, not us. It didn't make her any less furious, and it didn't make me feel any better that she no longer held us responsible.

I don't know how Rachel and Eva felt about all this, how they were coping with their mother's shaky return home. I saw less of the kids now—when they weren't in school, Jo and Chase and others took care of them while Rafi and I took turns caring for Maddie, trying to keep her from tipping over, while holding our hearts in our throats.

★ ★ ★

A few days later I was at my writing desk working on a story about a kid who steals a school bus. He'd just pulled out of the bus yard, his skinny arms stretched across the big steering wheel, thrilled to see the open road before him, when Rafi called.

"She's had another seizure," he said. "Come to the Brigham."

I grabbed my jacket and flew out the door: pure adrenaline, not a thought in my head. Like a fireman who hears the siren and jumps into action without registering fear or worry, some part of me was always on high alert in those years of Maddie's illness.

I found her in the ER, Rafi at her bedside. "Can you take over?" he said. "I have to go home to the girls."

I held her hand and tried to reassure her. She was stable but shaken. She'd been home all of four days, and she would never go home again.

I didn't know that at the time; I only knew that we weren't equipped to care for her at home. Here, at least, she'd be safe. It would be another week before I'd realize that her recovery had peaked a few days earlier, upon her release from the Spaulding. And now, before she'd even had a chance to enjoy her comeback, she was already sliding down the other side of the mountain.

★ ★ ★

They kept her at the Brigham only until they could find a placement for her at a long-term care facility. It all happened very quickly, and we found ourselves driving across the river to the Youville Hospital in Cambridge, just a mile from my house. A placid brick building surrounded by plants and trees. Inside, sparkling floors, the sharp smell of ammonia over a faint note of urine. She shared a room with a mostly invisible woman who appeared to be both ancient and in a vegetative state next to the window. Maddie's bed was close to the door, where staff could reach her easily.

★ ★ ★

I tried not to look at the other side of the room, which was easy to do because nothing was happening over there. Until now, Maddie had always had a single room in the hospital. This, her first roommate, could be mistaken for an unkempt blanket.

My stomach knotted. The walls of my denial were caving, but remarkably, I was able to plaster something over the studs before I lost all hope. In retrospect, I marvel at the terrific amount of energy that went into controlling my mind, keeping the bad stuff out, acknowledging—*feeling*—only a morsel of dread, no bigger than a tsetse fly.

It was May, 1991, almost four years since we'd first met.

★ ★ ★

I felt guilty that part of me breathed a sigh of relief that she was back in a hospital. The stress of having her at home, free to roam, but trapped in a body and mind that had become unglued, that peeled apart before your eyes, was agonizing. Those four days of her return home were among the hardest for me. Maybe we could fool ourselves while she was at the Spaulding, but back in her own home, it was impossible not to see how much was lost. In a hospital she looked pretty good. You could walk into a rehab hospital where the whole clientele is incapacitated, lying in their beds in varying degrees of *impossible*, and you could measure her improvement from day to day and week to week. But at home, the memory of how she'd moved through these rooms, gliding from kitchen to living room without a thought, the ease with which she'd lived in her body, the flow of her thoughts and her movements, was completely gone. The stark contrast between how she'd been at home just a few months ago, and how she struggled now, was brutal.

And oh, that helpless feeling of watching her rage against her own loss of autonomy. Her disbelief, her incomprehension of what had become of her.

Now at Youville, she didn't fight it, she rested. She could lie back and let it all go. Talk, listen, go for a spin in her wheelchair out to the courtyard. It was May and then it was June, the sun shone, there were birds and buds on the trees and the air was soft and sweet, blue sky dotted with cotton puffs of clouds that floated by.

This is ok, I remember thinking. *I can do this. We just coast along, this is fine.* Everything in order, predictable. The days sailing by without effort. *Up at 5:15, swim till 7, drive to Youville, spend an hour or two with Maddie, then the T to work. Rinse and repeat.* No surprises, no phone calls in the middle of the night, no emergencies, no struggles with schedules, no competition, no one to fight, nothing to push up against. A reprieve. Time to recover from the shock of the past few months, to regroup, to resign. A certain amount of resignation came with this new territory, and it did not feel sad or tragic; it felt peaceful, gentle, a relief. No expectations.

A grace period.

* * *

I was visiting Maddie as usual one morning soon after she arrived at Youville when, to my surprise, Rafi walked in. He never came to visit her during the day. He and I had pretty much divided our days so that I would take the morning and mid-day shifts at Maddie's bedside, and Rafi would visit in the evenings after work. "I asked him to come," Maddie said. "I need to speak to both of you. Together." Her voice was faint but clear. Rafi and I looked at each other and nodded dumbly.

Maddie's face had become more of a mask over the past week, and I couldn't read it. Nor could I tell what Rafi was thinking. Maddie had told him that she was in love with me two years ago, but I doubt she ever specifically said that we were *lovers*. I imagine some part of him must have known. Perhaps like Chase, he'd decided it was the tumor that loved me, not Maddie. I was no stranger to magical thinking and denial; I'd spent much of my life rearranging reality in order to keep a certain semblance of order and control in my mind. Perhaps none of that mattered now—whether Maddie and I were lovers, whether Rafi knew. All that really mattered was that she was still alive.

"Let's go for a walk," she said.

We helped her into the wheelchair and Rafi steered her down the corridor to the elevator. Down to the first floor and out to the courtyard. The sun was warm, the trees and grass impossibly green compared to her room.

"Listen," Maddie said, looking up at us. Her face was puffy, and she tilted slightly to one side, her eyes not quite focused. "I need you guys to set aside your differences and come together."

I was surprised by her directness, and from the look on Rafi's face, he, too, seemed momentarily taken aback. He looked at me and smiled tentatively.

Maddie took a deep breath. "It's just ... I can't choose," she said. "I need you both."

Rafi's smile grew warmer, and his whole face burst into blossom—a bristly blossom, for sure, but there was so much good will there. Above his granite cheekbones his dark shiny eyes disappeared into slits. He seemed on the verge of tears.

I, too, felt choked up, profoundly moved by this simple recognition of our importance to her.

"Besides," she said. "You're going to need each other."

At the time, Rafi and I only wanted to please her. We would have done swan dives out the window if she'd asked us to. After I returned home, I would marvel at how clearly Maddie had orchestrated this moment, catching us unawares and giving us permission to lay down our arms. Of course by then, Rafi and I were already much more accepting of each other, albeit still guarded. Our rivalry had become moot; what had separated him and me—Maddie—now bound us together.

We wheeled her back to her room, and settled her back into her bed. Rafi leaned over and kissed her on the forehead. "I have to go to the office," he said. "Hoolie will be with you."

He stood to go and smiled. "I'll call you later," he said to me. Like that, we had become teammates.

★ ★ ★

He called me at work a few hours later, and again in the afternoon after I'd spent my lunch break with her. I filled him in on how she was doing, and we agreed to talk again that night. "I'll be here from now on," he said. His film series would air in five months, and although he still had an enormous amount of writing and editing to do, his travels were over.

★ ★ ★

As the weeks slipped by, he and I talked daily. Often, we'd get together for supper with the girls at their apartment, or else Rafi would call me later at night, and we'd talk about our day, how Maddie was doing, the latest word from her doctors. The weaker Maddie got, the closer Rafi and I grew. Maddie was right; we did need each other. I looked forward to seeing him every day, hearing his voice, having someone to talk to about Maddie. We were in sync—as if we were holding her alive through our connection to each other.

Whenever I asked him about Rachel and Eva, he always said, "The kids are great." I understood that to mean that he was desperately grateful to have them, that he would go out of his mind without them, but that he probably didn't have a clue as to what they were feeling or how they were coping. I didn't either. When I was with them, the kids really did seem "great." They chatted about school and friends and their plans for the weekend. I didn't know how to ask them about their feelings. Was it my job? Wouldn't that be presumptuous of me? I wasn't qualified. I wasn't their parent. Looking back now, I wish I'd asked Rafi to arrange for them to talk to a therapist. Maybe he did; I don't know.

I didn't even know what I was feeling in those days.

"How are you holding up?" my own therapist asked me.

"I'm ok." I sounded surprisingly perky to myself.

Lisa looked at me with her calm blue eyes.

"Really. I'm doing ok."

"What would happen if you weren't ok?"

I looked at her, puzzled. "Nothing. I mean … What do you mean?"

"I'm just struck," she said, shifting her legs under her elegant jade green dress, "that you seem to need to be ok. When really, nothing about this situation is ok."

I nodded. She was never satisfied with my satisfaction. I knew that by now. But what did she want from me? "You mean you want me to feel *all* my feelings?"

She smiled. "That would be a start."

"I'm just taking this one day at a time. Right now, I'm ok." I was vaguely aware that I really didn't want to feel much of anything. Who willingly rolls out the welcome mat to pain? But it wasn't a matter of effort or will. My feelings were simply unavailable to me. (*The kids are great*, I could have said of myself.)

"A year ago, you used to say that when you left her side, you were suddenly filled with despair over her death. Is that still true?"

"No," I said, a little surprised at the realization. "I feel ok. Like I'm on cruise control."

She let my response hang in the air, until it sounded a bit flimsy and false, even to me. "I guess I used to be flooded by those feelings when she was relatively healthy. Now that she's actually dying, those feelings have fled."

We were quiet a moment while I wondered where they went.

"What else is going on in your life?"

What else? Wasn't this enough? I shrugged.

"What about work?"

I sighed. "We're in a fight with the bar advocates in the western part of the state. Turf wars. Nothing changes."

Lisa leaned back and cast her eyes up a moment before leveling her gaze at me. "I wonder where the rest of you is. Do you wonder about that at all? Do you feel like part of you is missing?"

I laughed. "You say that like it's a bad thing."

★ ★ ★

Where was the rest of me? Hiding in one of my compartments, I suppose. In those days I was not privy to the way my mind opened and closed doors, how it hustled my feelings from one hutch to another, keeping me in the dark. I was under a strict regime of Feelings Control, without even being conscious of it. Lisa was trying to pry open a few windows, let in a little light.

CHAPTER 18

In early June, I got word from our writing program that they were going to award Maddie her MFA at the July residency, despite her inability to teach a class. She'd knocked out all the other requirements with flying colors, had completed six semesters and seven residencies (two more than required); she'd written her thesis and dozens of stories and essays, and the quality of her work was excellent.

I rushed to the hospital to tell her. We'd spent the last three-and-a-half years dreaming of this, working toward this goal, and I was thrilled that her success was being honored by the program. I leaned over and kissed her forehead. "Hey kiddo," I said. "Good news from Warren Wilson."

Just this morning she'd managed to open her eyes and look at me when I first came in, but now her eyes were closed. I held her hand and leaned close to her ear to whisper the news, but she didn't respond. "Squeeze my hand if you can hear me."

Nothing.

"Maddie, you're being awarded the MFA."

Nothing. The silence in the room spooked me.

"Do you understand? They decided you've earned your MFA."

After a few moments, very faintly, I felt her squeeze my hand.

★ ★ ★

I drove home in turmoil, rattled by her silence. A silence in the exact shape of her, as if she had tunneled deep into herself, leaving a long thin trail of quiet accusation. Outside her room, the whispering footsteps of nurses in the hall, the faint blips of machines floating in the air. Inside her room, my heart pounded with the news of this strange immaculate silence.

And into that silence I now poured my worst fears as I sat in my Ford Escort waiting for the light to change at Mass Ave. Shame abhors a vacuum, and I leapt into that silence and found only judgment. I had failed her, I thought; I had put my own needs before hers. *What an idiot!* How could I have imagined she'd give a shit about her MFA? Here she was, on her deathbed, and somehow I'd thought she'd be happy to hear this news? I was shocked to realize that despite my wish for fusion, we were separated by a huge moat, and I lacked the will or imagination to cross it. I was still standing squarely in the land of the living, where such trinkets of achievement mattered. Shame on me! I knew better. *Nothing* mattered, really, but the next breath. Now, crossing Mass Ave and turning onto my street, I could hear her, in her shut-eyed silence, saying, *Really Hools? You need me to show enthusiasm for this? When do I get to stop taking care of you? All right, here, I'll squeeze your hand, are you happy now? Fine. Now go away and let me rest.*

★ ★ ★

It seems strange to me now that no one—neither Maddie, her family, Rafi, nor I, and not even their family lawyer, who made a house call in February before her last surgery to tweak her will—suggested drawing up a health care proxy or living will. Perhaps they did, and Maddie didn't want to deal with it. Over the years of her illness, I sometimes wondered what she felt about death—was she scared of dying? Did she imagine, like some people, that she might see her dead parents again? Or perhaps she pictured herself coming back as a dragonfly or songbird or mountain lion. I knew she wasn't religious, so I assumed that like me, she simply thought of death as a vast nothingness, a return to the elements. But I'd never asked her; I made myself wait till she raised the topic herself. She almost never did, and never for long. "I want to die at home," she once told me, maybe a year earlier. "Not in a hospital. But I know it's not possible—Rafi isn't built for that."

"What do you mean?"

"He just ... he wouldn't be able to do it. I know that about him—it's not how he's made." Her assessment sounded right to me. Rafi didn't strike me as someone comfortable around weakness or pain or disability. He seemed to want to leave caretaking to the caretakers, to doctors and nurses and womenfolk, while he went out and slayed dragons.

"But we can help him," I told her. We had a good network of family and friends who pitched in and helped with anything she needed. "We can help you die at home."

She was already shaking her head. "It's all right. I know him. He'll only feel worse. It doesn't matter." She never mentioned it again.

That's when I should have asked her *how* she wanted to die. But I didn't know the questions to ask, I'd never visited this territory before, and to be honest, didn't want to face it myself. I couldn't be the one to open that door until she did.

Looking back on this now of course, so many years later, after reading and drafting living wills and health care proxies, after making sure that "DNR" is written in all caps across my chart, I know the sorts of questions to ask. At what point would she no longer want medical intervention; under what circumstances would she prefer to die than be kept alive?

But the twelve weeks she was at the Spaulding, learning how to walk and talk again, all those hours we spent at her side, first wheeling her, and then walking with her down the long hallway to the windows overlooking the Charles River basin, we never spoke of death. We talked about recovering, about getting stronger, coming back to life. Her sole plan was to go home and to attend Rachel's school play.

And after those four short days at home, when another seizure plunged her back into the hospital, and her doctors tried to relieve the pressure in her brain by draining spinal fluids, we were too caught up in the flurry of emergencies to talk about death.

We should have broached the subject with her when she was transferred from the Brigham to Youville in early June, but we were exhausted and demoralized and it didn't occur to us. A week later, when she could no longer get into a wheelchair, when her downward slide from day to day was gradual but inevitable, when she finally lay propped in bed, attached to a catheter, no longer even in clothes anymore, but in a johnny, and we fed her bits of yogurt and applesauce, we didn't ask her.

And now it was too late. The day came in early June when she either couldn't or wouldn't eat any more. We held a baby spoonful of applesauce to her lips, but she didn't move a muscle. Even when we managed to get a little past her lips, it just sat there until we had to scoop it out so she wouldn't choke.

The doctor gathered us together in a small conference room—Rafi, Chase, brother-in-law Andy, and me—and asked us what we wanted to do. The room looked to have been dipped in beige and was 100 percent unnatural—polyester chairs, plasticated tabletop, synthetic walls.

I looked at Rafi. His brow was furrowed. Chase and Andy seemed calm. I took my cues from them.

"You have to decide whether you want us to put in a feeding tube," the doctor said gently. He was Pakistani, I think, with beautiful jet-black hair, dark skin and a soft voice. He seemed willing to spend all the time in the world with us.

"And if we don't?" Rafi asked.

The doctor nodded. "She'll die. Without food, her organs will slowly shut down and eventually she'll die."

"Is she suffering?"

He shook his head. "She's not in pain. We can always give her medication if she needs it."

"How much time do we have?"

He paused. I heard beeping sounds from somewhere down the hall. "She's still getting fluids through the IV, so she can probably live another couple of weeks without food. But you need to make the decision in the next day or two."

I'd never pictured this scene, that I'd be sitting around like a rational person, dispassionately discussing the specifics of the end of Maddie's life. What, exactly, *was* life? At the moment, I didn't wonder about the mystery of death; what concerned me now was the mystery of what was left of Maddie today. And tomorrow, and the next day. What were we clinging to, what were we unwilling to give up? Had Maddie already left us, by refusing to eat? She'd made her decision, shouldn't we honor it? But was she even capable of making a "decision" at all? She had stopped reacting to us, stopped squeezing our hands in response to questions.

What would she want, if she could speak?

Maddie was forty-three years old. She'd never smoked. She didn't drink, or not more than an occasional glass of wine at a party. She'd been active all her life—a runner and swimmer, who went to the gym and took aerobics, weightlifting, and dance classes. Her organs were brilliant—they could go on forever if she had a feeding tube providing her with nutrients. She could languish in this state of near oblivion for years, the doctor said. Her roommate, a faceless shape under a light blanket on the next bed, a Mrs. Somebody or Other, was on a feeding tube and had been kept alive like that for so long, her family didn't even bother to visit her anymore. She was a lump of living tissue on a hospital bed, whose liquids poured into her through a tube and poured out of her through another tube. It was almost as if she'd been planted there as a warning, a clear signal to us: *Do not go here.*

"Once you put a feeding tube in," the doctor explained, "it's harder to get it removed—from a legal, medical, and ethical standpoint. "So this is the critical juncture. We don't have to get any sort of outside approval simply *not* to insert a feeding tube. We're free to do nothing, and let her die in her own time.

"But if you decide to insert a feeding tube, then you have made a medical intervention to preserve her life. And if, at some point in the future, you want to remove the tube, it would be more difficult to do that. It would take a court order to approve it. It gets much more complicated later on."

He left the room to let us discuss it among ourselves.

"No feeding tube," I said to Rafi. At first he agreed. Her sister Chase and brother-in-law Andy also agreed, all of us nodding our heads like zombies.

"It's a no-brainer," we said with gallows humor. "She would not want to hang around in this condition for months or years."

But after we went home, Rafi began to doubt himself. Time was running out, and he called me that evening. "I don't think I can let her go yet," he said. "If we don't give her a feeding tube, it would be like killing her, wouldn't it? I don't think I can do that."

I winced, queasy to think he could even *consider* inserting a feeding tube.

It occurs to me now that Rafi's decision was particularly hard for him because his entire family had been killed in the Holocaust; *Nazis* were killers, not him! How could he be asked to kill his own wife? Maddie and the girls were all he had left in the world.

"No, Rafi," I said, trying to keep the alarm out of my voice. "We'd be *letting her* die. Not killing her. There's a difference."

Rafi was quiet. A pair of finches made a fuss outside my window in a square of light. It was early June, summer was just beginning to spread her wings, the days were long, and Maddie would never be outside again.

"But it's not about us," I said. "It's about her. What would she want?"

She would never feel the sun on her skin again. Never feel the breeze.

I felt certain she wouldn't want the feeding tube. No one in my family would. *There are many worse things than death*, my parents had always told me. Having lived through genocide and famine, typhus and cholera, they were experts on life and death. Death, they said, was a mercy for anyone in an irreversible persistent vegetative state.

Which was where Maddie was now.

What would *she* want?

"I don't know," Rafi said. "I mean, I thought I knew, but now I'm not so sure. She never said what she would want. Did she ever talk with you about it?"

"No, she avoided any mention of the end. But I'm pretty sure she wouldn't want to live like this. I mean, she's never coming back, the cancer *will* kill her, but it could take months or even years." I was just repeating what the doctor had told us.

"I don't think I can do it," he said. "I think we should give her the feeding tube."

I felt my stomach clench, as if I were the one getting the feeding tube. I saw us marching across a vast empty desert with no end in sight. Maybe I needed a landmark, an end post, a finish line. Maybe it was my own weakness, my own inability to hang in limbo that made me want to let her go, to cut her loose. To cut *me* loose. I couldn't bear to prolong the wasteland.

It wasn't my call; it was Rafi's. He was her husband. This was just one more reminder of how marginal I really was. I was the lover, I occupied the *closet* of Maddie's heart.

★ ★ ★

If I'd been in Rafi's place—if the final decision had rested on my shoulders—would I have had a harder time reaching a decision? I don't think so. For whatever reason, I felt certain that Maddie would not have wanted to linger like this with a feeding tube. But who can really speak for another person? In the end I could only be sure that *I* wouldn't want to linger like this.

Still, it was strange to find myself—a remarkably immature and sheltered thirty-three-year-old—now assuring Rafi that Maddie would want to die. I knew nothing, yet I argued with the unearned confidence of the self-righteous.

"I just don't think I can do it," he said.

We hung up. I began to panic in earnest. I called a lawyer friend and asked him a hypothetical:

(a) If a husband decides to have a feeding tube inserted in his wife who is in a vegetative state as a result of a brain tumor, but otherwise healthy, what rights do the patient's siblings or other family members have to contest it? (I knew, of course, that as her lover and friend, I had none.)

(b) If the tube is inserted, and the husband subsequently changes his mind weeks or months later, what legal obstacles would have to be overcome in order to remove the tube at that time?

My friend is an excellent lawyer, so his answers to both questions were exactly what I'd expected: *It depends.*

And it was precisely this uncertainty that I found so terrifying. I preferred the inevitability of Maddie's death to this enormous unruly question mark hovering over our heads, the prospect of a never-ending limbo for her. After a two-and-a-half-year roller coaster ride, I wanted a small measure of control—the chance, finally, to apply the brakes and disembark.

Rafi called me a few more times over the next two days, trying to figure out what Maddie would want. At last he agreed: no feeding tube. He didn't say why he changed his mind, and I didn't ask. I was simply relieved by his decision. I don't know if he had talked about it with anyone else. He was not a touchy-feely guy, and had no use for therapy. Maddie once told me that over the years of their marriage, whenever she'd tried to get him to talk about his feelings, he'd simply fallen asleep instead.

I, on the other hand, was a talker. I spent a session talking with Lisa about it, and I may have surprised her with my complete lack of doubt on the subject. I talked with Anita, and told her that Maddie had stopped eating. True to form, Anita was tactful, sympathetic, and did not pry. "I'm so sorry," she said.

★ ★ ★

There's something very clarifying about death: it puts everything in stark perspective. The things that used to make you crazy seemed silly now. Who cares, I thought, if Rafi fucked other women? Who cares if he could be a bombastic bully? In those final months of Maddie's life, I also doubt that Rafi cared whether I'd fucked his wife, whether I'd sprinkled lesbian vibes around his kids; or that I spouted shallow leftie opinions and represented guilty people. Dying is a powerful measuring stick. Nothing else can come close to mattering.

Of course the rest of the world crashes in on you eventually, reminding you that a lot of things do matter. Climate change, racism, misogyny, homophobia, inequality, violence, human rights, freedom—it's all there waiting for you to take up arms again. But in that bubble of time around Maddie's death, I didn't have the energy to care. For months afterwards, all that mattered was staying close to Rafi and the girls. They were the closest thing I could get to Maddie. They would be my bridge to the rest of my life.

CHAPTER 19

After Rafi made the decision not to insert a feeding tube, I continued to visit Maddie every morning after my swim. I kissed her forehead, held her hand, and sat next to her for an hour, talking about whatever was on my mind, or just sat in silence with her before heading downtown to work. A week went by like that, then a second. I began to think that maybe she was made of magic, that she could go on forever, that the feeding tube was a non-issue. She would live on nothing but fluids and air. Every day before leaving, I kissed her good-bye and whispered, "See you tomorrow," making sure to take stock of this moment, memorizing her face, reminding myself that this might be the last time I would see her alive.

The next day everything was exactly the same.

Except now a growing parade of family and friends came to say good-bye. One after another they shuffled in and either stood at the foot of her bed or touched her arm and whispered words. Some cried. I found this almost unbearable. Aside from Maddie's extended family and Israeli friends, I didn't want all these people in her room.

"Why not?" Lisa asked.

"I don't know. They get in my way."

"You want her for yourself."

Selfish! I couldn't deny it—I liked talking to Maddie alone, telling her about my day. I was too self-conscious to do that in front of other people. But it was more than that. "It just ... it

bugs me. All these people I've never even seen before now showing up and subjecting Maddie to some creepy deathbed scene.
Like some Russian novel where all the characters come to 'pay
their respects.'"

"Well she is on her deathbed," Lisa said. "So they're getting
in the way of your denial."

That stopped me. "What? No, it's not like that."

She nodded. "What's it like?"

"It just seems like such a big production. The more people
come, the more detached I feel. I have to leave the room; I can't
witness it, it's too weird. It interferes with my relationship with
Maddie. They don't belong there."

Lisa's voice was very gentle. "Things are changing."

It's true. I'd had a routine. And I was good with my routine,
it was working for me, but now there were all these people I had
to interact with. "The only person who understands me is Rafi,"
I said. "No one else makes any sense to me at all." My fear that
Rafi would insert a feeding tube was ancient history. We were
completely back in sync now.

Lisa's eyes were a soothing blue. I had to look away so I
wouldn't cry. "Maddie knew it," I said, smiling at the thought.
"She set us up."

Lisa tilted her head quizzically.

"Maddie's been trying to get me and Rafi together for
months. Since ... All spring." Rafi had told me she'd been pres-
suring him, too, urging him to reach out to me. "And she was
right. I can't do without him."

Lisa nodded.

The last four months had transformed my relationship with
my lover's husband.

"And you know what else bugs me?" I said. "All these friends
of hers? They're all so *emotional*. Like all of a sudden it dawns

on them that she's dying." For two-and-a-half years, nothing, and now, *boom*, they're bawling their heads off."

"What about you?" Lisa asked. "Where's your grief?"

I looked at her blankly.

I don't remember if Rafi brought the girls to see Maddie one last time. If he did, I wasn't there. I was holding myself in suspense, barely touching the ground. I followed my routine—sleep, swim, visit Maddie, go to work, talk to Rafi, talk to Rafi, talk to Rafi. Go to his place, have dinner with him and the kids, go home, go to sleep …

Until one morning after my swim, I walked down the hall to her room and saw Rafi standing in the corridor in tears.

I blinked. That couldn't be right; Rafi was never here at this time. I kept walking and he kept being there.

We said nothing. He wrapped me in a big bear hug, and we sobbed together. He was shaking; it was like being held in the arms of an earthquake. He led me down the hall to a large room furnished with pale blue chairs and couches. Rachel and Eva ran to me, and we held each other and cried. Rafi joined us, and we formed a great glob of grief in the middle of the room. In the midst of my grief, I felt so grateful to have them to hold onto, so grateful to be included as part of their family. Behind them I saw Chase and her husband Andy, calm and cool-headed, conferring over a long list of people to notify. Andy went out to the pay phone and returned for more names and numbers. Chase, too, went out to call family and friends. I was amazed and a little unnerved by their composure, their ability to function as adults, while Rafi and I and the girls were bawling our heads off, clinging to each other, unable to speak, much less dial a number.

Those feelings that I couldn't find any trace of in therapy? Here they were. The floodgates had opened.

She'd died on the summer solstice. Chase and her husband took care of all the arrangements—cremation followed by a graveside burial of her ashes at the Mt. Auburn cemetery. She would rest in her family plot, next to her father and mother, their simple dark gravestones laid flush with the earth. A beautiful spot under the arms of an ancient something tree, off the beaten path, very soothing.

Too soothing. Too quiet.

We had four days before the funeral. I spent them with Rafi and the kids, deciding what we would say at her graveside. Eva chose to read John Donne's "Death Be Not Proud." She practiced the lines in her clear angelic voice. I was in awe—and a little intimidated—that an eleven-year-old could recite such a poem. I had a hard enough time just understanding it.

Death, be not proud, though some have called thee

Mighty and dreadful, for thou are not so;

For those whom thou think'st thou dost overthrow

Die not, poor Death, nor yet canst thou kill me ...

I chose an excerpt from an Eleanor Wilner poem, "Search Party," but when the time came, I could barely choke out the words.

... As if all death were counterfeit,

all silence, sham—shattered by the racket of the heart:

give back, give back, give back

we shouted at the sky ...

The sky was in fact flawless on the day of her funeral—sparkling blue as if freshly laundered. A few dozen friends and family in bright dresses and summer slacks walked the winding road from the gated entrance of the Mt. Auburn Cemetery through gentle hills of ancient oaks and maples, dotted with hemlock and spruce. A chorus of catalpa and mountain laurel spilled their blossoms. It was like walking through an enchanted forest, so it came as a shock to arrive at the freshly dug hole where Maddie's ashes would rest.

Rafi didn't speak at all; he couldn't. He clung to the girls, and I clung to one of Maddie's closest friends who had quickly become mine, too. Fountains of tears. Chase's husband Andy was the master of ceremonies. It was a simple, quiet, lovely burial that ripped me in two. Afterwards we trooped back to Rafi's place to eat and drink with family and friends who milled about, chatting and laughing. Platters of food materialized: deli meats and cheeses, bread, fruit, sweets. Chase must have arranged for everything with the seemingly effortless serenity for which she was famous. How strange, I thought: we're having a *party*. I had no appetite, but took a glass of wine and held onto it as if it might save my life. It did. Soon I was talking with one of Maddie's friends, then another and another ... It felt surreal, all those things we do around death. All those motions and rituals, all that structure, containers for feelings.

★ ★ ★

The summer writing program residency kicked off in early July, a few weeks after her funeral. I flew down to Swannanoa without Maddie for the first time. I'd graduated in January and this was my eighth time back. I didn't attend the whole residency; I just came for the last day and night, to give Maddie's graduate reading and to accept her MFA for her at the graduation ceremony.

Reuniting with our writer friends from all over the country was like being swept up in a great river of love. Everyone had stories about Maddie, and we shared our memories, laughter, and tears. Maddie and I had bonded over our writing; this was our community, and now our friends gathered and filled the gaps between us with words.

On the final night of the residency, I read a section of Maddie's essay about her experiences in "the outer space of living with brain tumors." Her faculty supervisor had suggested the topic at the January residency six months ago, when her mind had already begun to falter. Maddie had titled the essay "Memoirs of an Amnesiac." It was the last piece she ever wrote.

I worried that I'd botch it, that I'd break down, collapse into a puddle of tears, but when I stood at the podium and looked out at our motley group of fifty or sixty writing friends and colleagues, I felt at home. Maddie's words on the page seemed to rise through my body and out of my mouth:

"In writing all of this, I want to do justice to what my head has gone through. This horrid experience has been an experience, the tumor is, maybe, a gift of meaning to my life and to what I want to write. The dreadful irony is that this Indian giver may someday take away any ability of mine to understand meaning."

She was with me, she was beaming out at the crowd. Toward the end of my reading I glanced up to see a silky black cat promenade down the aisle of the auditorium like a fashion model. Stately, elegant, fluid. I knew it was Maddie, coming toward the stage for her final round of applause.

★ ★ ★

For the rest of that summer, when I wasn't at work I stayed basically glued to Rafi and the kids, spending weekends at their place, getting together for supper. Sometimes we drove down to Westport to hang out with Maddie's cousins who had converted an old barn into a shambling outpost on an inlet. They enlisted us to join in a neighborhood softball game one weekend on their mown field; while we played, someone threw burgers on a grill. Home-baked pies lay spread across the picnic table, waiting to be ravished. I moved as if in a dream, feeling safe only when I was close to Rafi and the kids.

And then, little by little, the impossible and inevitable process of weaving ourselves back into our lives began.

★ ★ ★

It wasn't until the following year, when I was home for Thanksgiving in 1992, that I finally told my mother I was gay.

"You don't know," she said calmly. We were sitting together on the little sofa in the TV room after watching a videotape of "To Sir With Love."

"Mom, Maddie and I were more than friends; we were lovers."

Her eyes widened but she recovered quickly. "Maddie was an artist," she reasoned. "That's understandable."

I felt a slight sting at my mother's distinction of Maddie as an artist, while dismissing me as a pathetic wannabe.

"Mom, I'm trying to be honest with you, ok? I've known for a long time. I didn't want to tell you because I didn't want to hurt you." I fought back tears. "Maddie and I were lovers. I loved her. She loved me."

My mother drew back. Her eyes narrowed, as if by sheer galactic Mom Vision, she could telepathically steer me away from the Homosexual Box and back to the Normal Box where I belonged. "Well, then you did it for her sake. She was dying. You did it as a kindness."

I said nothing, giving my mother time to absorb my information. She already knew my sister was gay, but she couldn't imagine that I was, too.

"Maddie and I were in love, Mom. It wasn't a kindness. It was love."

But I was thinking: Was kindness more honorable than love? If I was in love, did that make me less kind?

EPILOGUE

The two and a half years I'd spent at Maddie's side as she underwent four gruesome brain operations—the last one from which she'd had to learn to walk and talk again, only to die months later—was a sort of crucible for me. I had thrown myself whole-heartedly into the burning building of a love affair promising agony and certain death. I had valiantly (and perhaps foolishly) stayed at her side in the hospital room marked with radioactive signs prohibiting visitors while she lay for days in isolation with a radiation implant in her frontal lobe. If I could not save her, I wanted to be as close to her as possible through her two-and-a-half-year ordeal.

At times I felt I would never recover from Maddie's death, and sometimes I wished I hadn't. But in some twisted way, I also earned a margin of self-respect. In my family, suffering built character. My parents' survival of atrocities had made them immense, all-powerful. They used their power to protect me from the dangers of the world, thereby—ironically—ensuring my status as someone for whom they (and I) had no respect.

Maybe losing Maddie had given me something of what they had—a loss so profound that life seemed pointless afterwards. I was no longer the innocent they had protected from the cruelties of the world. It was Maddie who taught me about death, about losing what you most love, and it was Rafi who taught me about moving forward, about forgiving yourself and others, and living.

* * *

Over the years after Maddie's death, Rafi and I drifted apart and saw less and less of each other. I eventually fell in love with that most elusive of creatures—an unmarried lesbian!—and Rafi and the girls came over to meet her. We got together once in a while, but then time shot ahead, the girls grew up, Rafi eventually retired and took up his dream of sailing around the world.

Until one day, at the age of seventy-five, illness cut his trip short. He flew back to Boston with his girlfriend and was diagnosed with end-stage pancreatic cancer with only months to live. His daughters Rachel and Eva, now in their thirties, called to let me know when I could come visit him.

It was a sunny day in April, 2017, when I walked down their street. The trees along the sidewalk showed off their bright green leaves. I entered the brownstone and climbed the three flights of stairs to their apartment. His daughters greeted me at the door, and we hugged. I was stunned by how tall and drop-dead gorgeous they were. Like Maddie, they seemed utterly unaware of their beauty.

We walked down the hallway to the bedroom—the same light-filled room where I'd spent so much time at Maddie's side over a quarter-century earlier. Now, for the first time, I saw Rafi in the bed. He'd lost weight but looked good, and I felt overcome by happiness to see him. He sat up when I came in and his face brightened. "Hoolie!" he said with a big shit-eating grin. "You got old!"

He died a week later.

* * *

My wife Donna and I went to his funeral at the Mount Auburn Cemetery on a day as gloriously warm and sunny as the day we'd buried Maddie nearly twenty-six years earlier. I could feel Maddie on my shoulder as I greeted Rafi's and Maddie's family and friends, and for a moment, time seemed to have folded in on itself. Here we all were again, older, grayer, but with new shoots of life that Maddie had never known: Rachel's and Eva's husbands and kids—Maddie's grandchildren. The four young boys ran loops around their parents, bright white shirts and silk neckties coming loose and untucked. Maddie would have been delighted. I could feel her smiling though my own lips.

★ ★ ★

What were the chances that I would meet a woman in a writing workshop in Cambridge, Massachusetts in 1987—a woman married to a Jewish survivor from *my parents' hometown*? A woman who, like me, didn't discover her own mother's secret Jewish identity until she was in her thirties? A woman who was becoming aware of her attraction to women just as I was about to embrace my identity as a Jew? Our love affair was complicated not only by cancer, homophobia, and adultery, but also by a history of the Holocaust, anti-Semitism and transgenerational trauma; by deeply held secrets and shame.

Maddie had always pushed me to do what scared me most, to seek my truth, to be whoever I was. She had started me on this journey, Rafi carried me through, cheering me on through the years of research to write the story of my family's history. Both of them offered me a sense of family before I'd even been able to understand my own.

The strands of our stories weave in and out, connecting us in ways that make our lives seem implausible—we're all linked by our narratives, and we learn who we are through our connections and interactions with one other.

I often wish that Maddie had lived long enough to find out that she'd been right all along about me. I'd like to think she knew that she'd led me to discover not only who I am, but also that I *don't mind* being who I am.

This was a gift that I hadn't expected. I hadn't even known it was possible.

# # #

Photo credit: Mikki Ansin

ABOUT THE AUTHOR

HELEN FREMONT is the author of the national bestseller *After Long Silence*. Her second memoir, *The Escape Artist*, was selected as an "Editor's Choice" by *The New York Times*. Her work has appeared in numerous publications, including *Prize Stories: The O. Henry Awards*, *The New York Times*, *Ploughshares*, and *The Harvard Review*. She has been a teaching fellow at both Bread Loaf and the Radcliffe Institute. She was a Scholar in the Women's Studies Research Center Scholars Program at Brandeis University and worked as a public defender in Boston, where she now lives with her wife. You can find Helen online at HelenFremont.com.

ACKNOWLEDGMENTS

Several small villages of friends, mentors, colleagues, and professional geniuses helped me write this book. First of all, Gail Hochman is magic. Her generosity and giant heart have carried me over countless obstacles over the years. I am not only grateful, but forever in awe.

Thanks to Vicki DeArmon, a veritable force of nature; Julia Park Tracey, a multi-talented, organizational wizard; Suzy Vitello, Editor Extraordinaire; Alicia Feltman, gifted artist and designer; and the entire kick-ass crew at Sibylline Press. Just wow.

I am enormously grateful to the MFA Program for Writers at Warren Wilson College, and in particular, Ellen Bryant Voigt, the mastermind, spark, and genius who founded it as the first low-residency MFA program in the country. I am equally amazed and grateful to the faculty, students, and alumni who continually brought me back from the brink and into the light. Thanks in particular to my teachers and mentors, including Charles Baxter, Stephen Dobyns, Allan Gurganus, C.J. Hribal, Margot Livesey, Michael Martone, Mary Elsie Robertson, Richard Russo, Joan Silber, John Skoyles, and Eleanor Wilner.

Helen Epstein has been not only a good friend, but also a consistently encouraging, demanding, uplifting, and smart writing partner. Mari Coates, Nan Cuba, Trish Hampl, Michael Laughlan, Alison Moore, Eric Rampson, Katherine Rooks, and Susan Sterling: thank you for reading early drafts and for inspiring and commiserating with me as writers and dear friends. I don't have room to list you all, but my gratitude is boundless.

To my P2P writing group—Wallies all—who have nourished me, taken me under their collective wing, swung me around the dance floor, scraped me off the pavement, and offered me First

Aid, not only for my writing, but also for my frequently rumpled heart and soul: Lynette D'Amico, Genanne Walsh, Tracy Winn, and Stan Yarbro, thanks for being my posse. I'd also like to honor the memory of Geoff Kronik, who was a beloved member of our group. His friendship, extraordinary talent, and help with early sections of this book were invaluable to me.

I don't know where I'd be without Nancy Gist and her ferocious support, her zany humor, and that rarest of commodities: good sense. Thanks to my friends and colleagues at CPCS for their commitment to fighting for human rights and criminal justice, for including me on their team, and for putting up with me when I was off scribbling and getting an MFA.

Unfettered thanks to the WISW and the entire gang of rowers, swimmers, and other lunatics who regularly push me to my anaerobic threshold and follow up with feasts of equal excess.

Lisa McElaney and Abe Morell have been, and continue to be, my lifeline. As part of Maddie's close circle of loved ones, they have taken me in as their own, and broadened my sense of family.

I am forever grateful to Lisa Rubinstein for steering me through the last forty or so years of dreck, keeping a steady hand on the wheel, a magnanimous heart, profound wisdom, and an excellent sense of direction. Without her, it's doubtful I would have ever figured out how to be in a relationship in the first place.

Thanks to Maddie's family, who know who they are. I feel deeply honored and grateful to them for opening their hearts to me and teaching me what matters.

Finally, all my gratitude and wonder to Donna—my love and light, who always carries my books for me.

STUDY GUIDE QUESTIONS

1. How we see ourselves in the world—our sense of self—changes over time. How does Helen's understanding of herself change over the course of the book? How does Maddie's?

2. Think about experiences in your own life that have dramatically threatened or altered your understanding of who you are. What have you learned about yourself and others as a result?

3. Secrets, shame and betrayal: nearly all of the main characters in the book are hiding parts of themselves, either consciously or unconsciously, in order to conform to cultural, familial, and societal pressures. What do the characters gain and lose by presenting a false front to others?

4. What does it mean for Maddie and Helen when they agree that they can, in effect, break all the rules? Are they actually free to behave and act on their feelings? To what extent must they continue to comport themselves within the lines of propriety? What would happen if they didn't?

5. Think of the times in your own life when you have had to choose between your need to be true to yourself, and your need to accommodate the wishes or needs of others. How did you resolve these conflicts within yourself? Would you choose differently now?

6. How does a terminal illness change one's priorities and assumptions about how to live? How does Helen's alternating

acceptance of, and denial of, impending death affect her and Maddie's relationship?

7. Have you ever had to face the imminent death of a loved one? Absent explicit discussion or directions, how would you decide the point at which a loved one would want to be allowed to die? Why didn't Helen, Maddie, and her family address this issue sooner?

Sibylline Press is proud to publish the brilliant work of women authors over 50. We are a woman-owned publishing company and, like our authors, represent women of a certain age.